SALVADOR DALÍ

DISCOVERING ART

The Life, Times and Work of the World's Greatest Artists

SALVADOR DALÍ

O. B. DUANE

BROCKHAMPTON PRESS

This book is dedicated to Nora Butler, my muse in troubled times.

First published in Great Britain by Brockhampton Press,
an imprint of The Caxton Publishing Group,
20 Bloomsbury Street, London WC1B 3JH

ISBN 1 84186 090 5

Produced by Flame Tree Publishing,
The Long House, Antrobus Road, Chiswick, London W4 5HY
for Brockhampton Press
A Wells/McCreeth/Sullivan Production

Pictures printed courtesy of the Visual Arts Library, London, and Edimedia, Paris,
and with thanks to the Estate of Salvador Dalí, and DACS.

Printed and bound by Oriental Press, Dubai

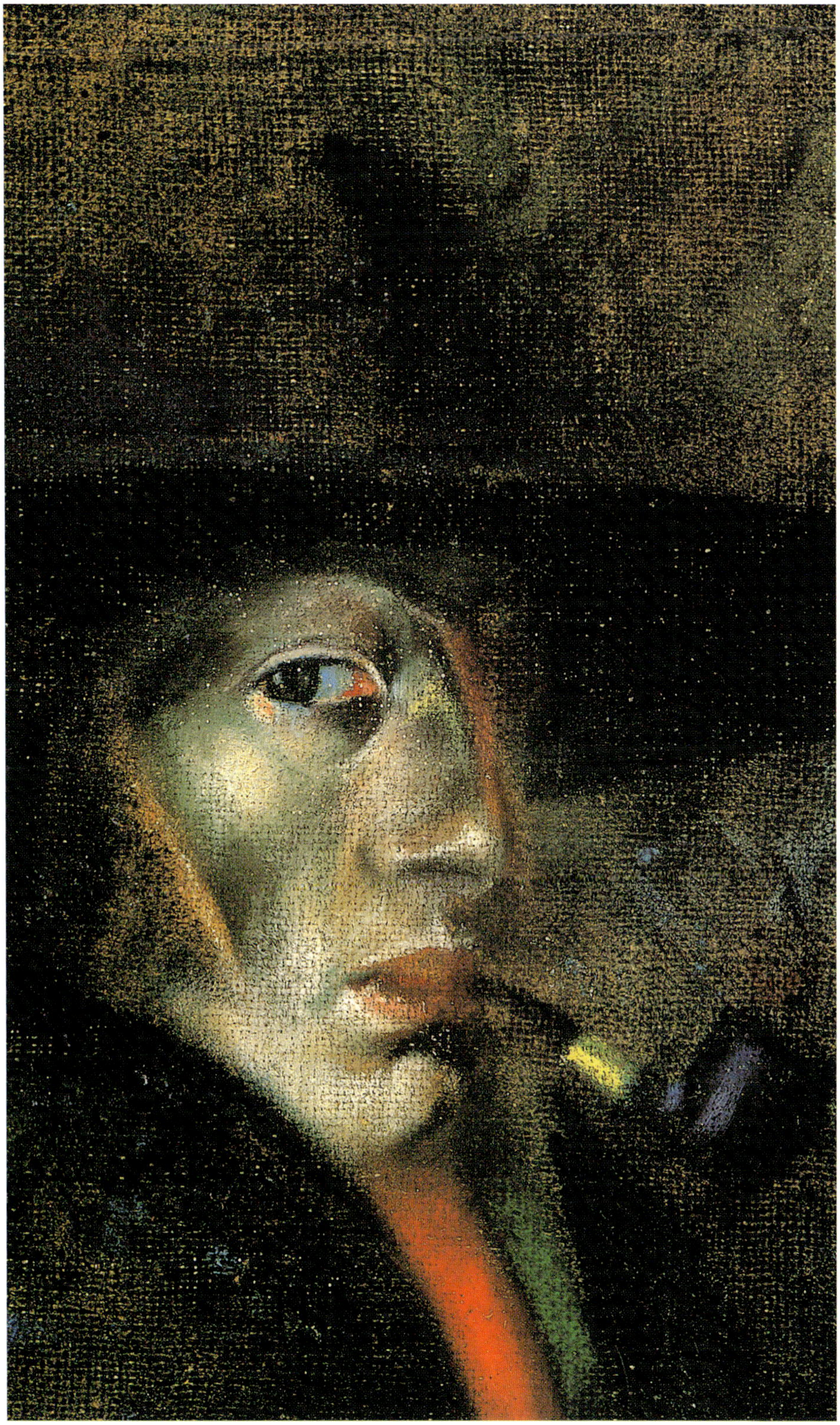

CONTENTS

Chronology 6

The Making of an Idol 8

The Sovereign of Surrealism 26

Gala-Dalí and Port Lligat 42

The Later Works 62

Index 80

Selection of Prints 81

Self-Portrait, Figueres, 1921 (Gala y Salvador Foundation, Figueres). Dalí painted this self-portrait when he was seventeen, as he was about to enter the San Fernando Academy in Madrid. His work at this time was still heavily influenced by Impressionism. Oil on canvas. 36.8 x 41.9 cm

CHRONOLOGY

1904 Salvador Dalí is born on 11 May in Figueres.

1918 First exhibition of his work held at the Municipal Theatre in Figueres.

1921 Dalí's mother dies. He enters the San Fernando Academy of Fine Arts in Madrid where he meets Federico Garcia Lorca and Luis Buñuel.

1923 He criticizes his lecturers and is suspended.

1925 Dalí spends his holidays at Cadaqués with Garcia Lorca. First solo exhibition at the Dalmau gallery in Barcelona.

1926 Dalí travels to Paris for the first time; meets Picasso. Expelled from the Madrid Academy.

1927 Publishes *Saint Sebastian,* dedicated to Lorca, and *Film-arte, fil antiartístico.*

1928 Dalí writes 'The Yellow Manifesto' with Lluís Montañya and Sebastià Gasch.

1929 In the spring, Dalí is in Paris to film *Un Chien Andalou.* Through Miró, he meets many leading Surrealists. Paul Eluard visits Cadaqués in the summer and Dalí falls in love with Gala. First exhibition in Paris at the Goemans Gallery.

1930 Begins to develop his paranoiac-critical theory. In *Le Surréalisme au service de la révolution* he publishes *L'Âne pourri,* and in the *Editions Surréalistes* his *La Femme visible.* He buys a fisherman's cottage at Port Lligat near Cadaqués.

1931 His first one-man exhibition held at the Pierre Colle Gallery in Paris. He also publishes *L'Amour et la Mémoire.*

1932 Dalí exhibits in the first Surrealist show in the USA and has a second one-man exhibition. He writes *Babaouo,* a screenplay, but the film is never made.

1935 *Conquest of the Irrational* is published in New York.

1936 The Spanish Civil War begins. Dalí lectures at the International Exhibition of Surrealism in London and appears on the cover of *Time* magazine.

1938 He visits Freud in London and works on two ballets in Monte Carlo.

1939 The breach with the Surrealists is now final. In the USA Dalí publishes *Declaration of the Independence of the Imagination and the Rights of Man to His Own Madness.* He works on *Dream of Venus* for New York World's Fair.

1940 Dalí and Gala return to the USA where they remain in exile until 1948.

1942 *The Secret Life of Salvador Dalí* is published in America.

1948 He publishes *Fifty Secrets of Magic Craftsmanship* and *Hidden Faces.*

1949 Dalí and Gala return to Europe and he paints *The Madonna of Port Lligat.*

1951 Dalí publishes *The Mystical Manifesto.* His particle period begins.

1960 Dalí paints epic-format mystical works such as *The Ecumenical Council.*

1961 The *Ballet de Gala* is premiered in Venice, with libretto and set design by Dalí. He exhibits his first 'historical picture', *The Discovery of America by Christopher Columbus.*

1963 Dalí publishes *The Tragic Myth of Millet's Angelus.*

1964 A first major Dalí retrospective is held at the Seibu Museum, Tokyo. Dalí publishes *Diary of a Genius* and is awarded one of the highest decorations in Spain.

1968 *Les Passions selon Dalí,* with Louis Pauwels, is published in Paris.

1970 *Dalí by Dalí* is published in New York.

1971 The Salvador Dalí Museum is opened in Cleveland, Ohio.

1977 An exhibition of Dalí's latest works is held at André-François Petit Gallery in Paris, including *Gare de Perpignan.*

1982 Gala dies and Dalí becomes Marques de Pubol.

1983 Dalí paints his last picture, *Swallowtail.*

1988 First Dalí exhibition in the Soviet Union is held at the Pushkin Museum, Moscow.

1989 Dalí dies of heart failure at the age of eighty-five.

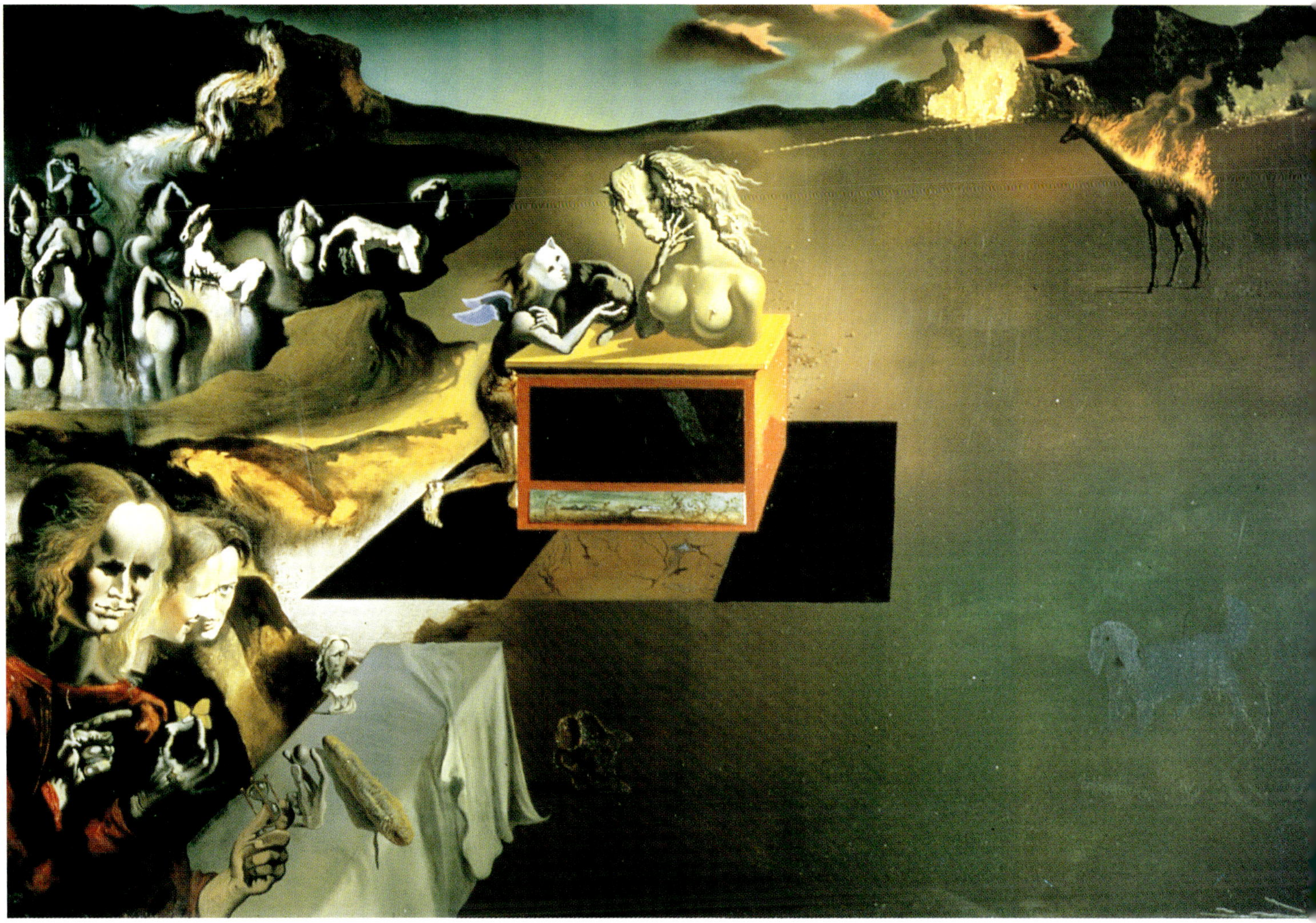

The Invention of Monsters, 1937 (Chicago Art Institute). A great number of the canvases Dalí produced in exile from Spain during the Civil War show the influence of Renaissance Masters. He employs groups of figures, painted in a variety of styles, to establish multiple images. Oil on canvas. 51 x 78 cm

CHAPTER 1

The Making of an Idol

Every morning upon awakening, I experience a supreme pleasure: that of being Salvador Dalí, and I ask myself, wonder-struck, what prodigious thing will he do today, this Salvador Dalí.

Diary of a Genius

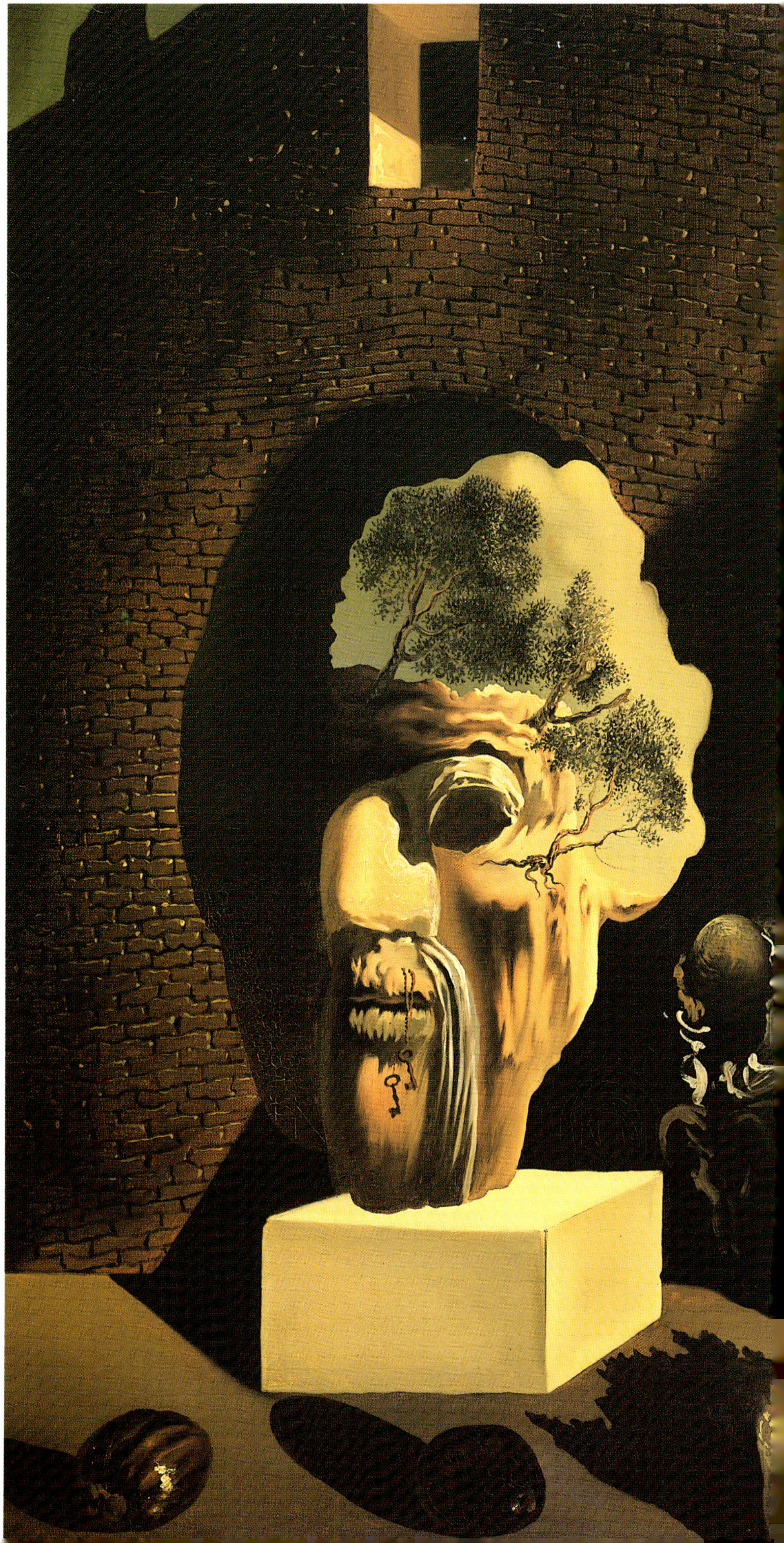

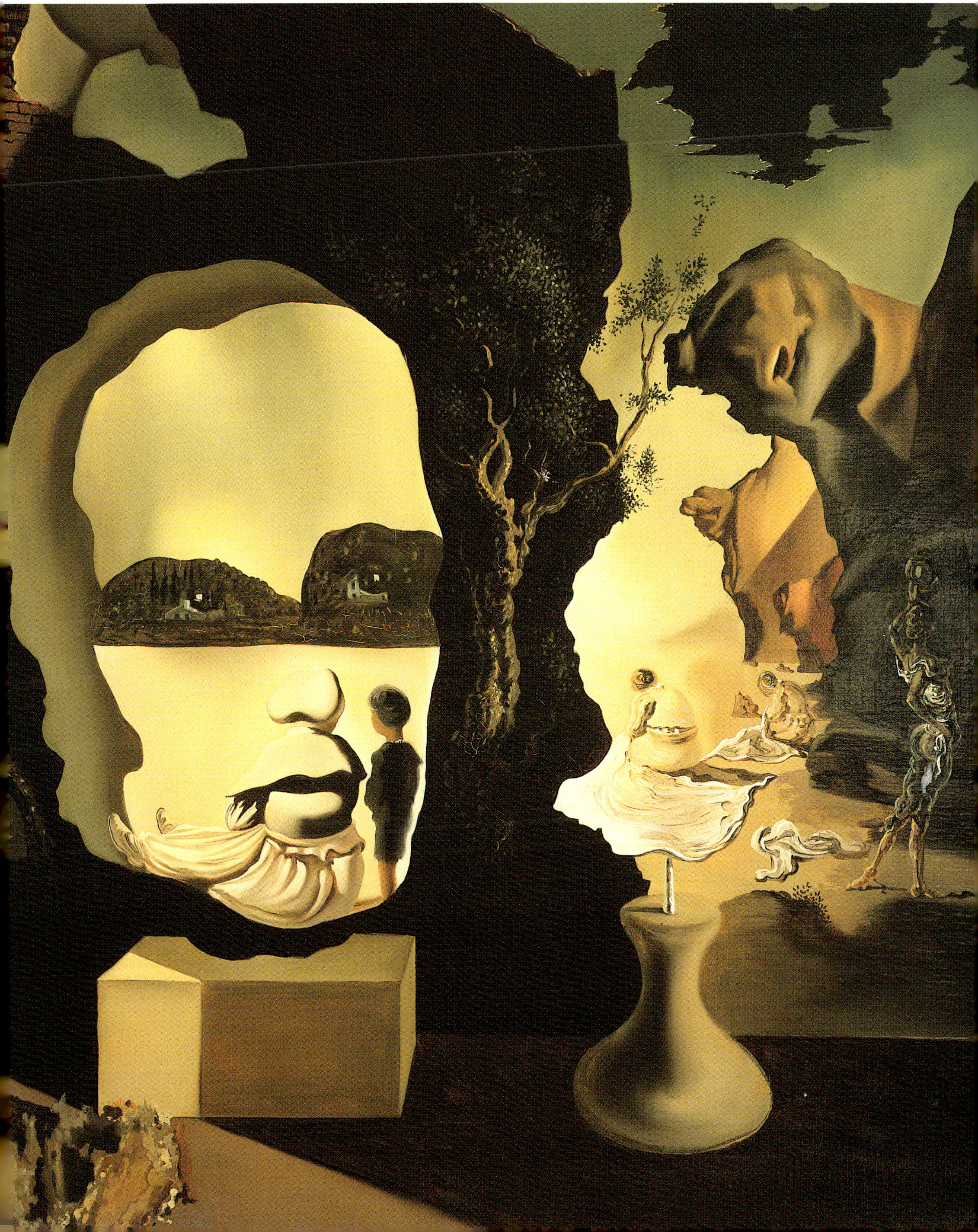

Overleaf:
Old Age, Adolescence, Infancy (The Three Ages), 1940 (Salvador Dalí Museum, St Petersburg, Florida). Many of the familiar elements of Dalí's work are present here. The heads representing the ages are double images. They are holes in a vast brick wall of time through which can be seen the landscape of Cadaqués, the cypress tress, the rocks of Cape Creus and the small boy in the sailor suit who is Dalí himself. Oil on canvas. 49.8 x 65 cm

Dalí's entire life was marked by the profound desire to assert his individuality. His unique personality, basking in the most extreme activity at every possible opportunity, has been discussed, criticized and analyzed as part of the universal attempt to unravel the frequently daunting complexity of his work. Even today, seventy-five years after Dalí's first paintings emerged, opinion is divided on the issue of his artistic genius. There are many who refute it, denouncing his 'indefinable' canvases as the work of a conman. Others eulogize over his immense talents, applauding the challenge to traditional critical interpretation his paintings have presented over the years. No other twentieth-century artist, with the possible exception of Pop Art's Andy Warhol, has provoked such a highly controversial response. Dalí's work is either admired or detested. His world is uncompromising, strange and fascinating. It demands, above all other things, an adventurous and permissive spirit, eager to brave the unknown.

A great deal of light may be shed on Dalí's art through an exploration of his background. He was a man inextricably bound to his native Catalonia, to his family and to his past, especially his childhood and adolescence which remained absolutely crucial to him. Catalonia shaped him, nurtured him, infuriated him, frustrated him, yet utterly consumed him. Dalí could never entertain the thought of leaving his birthplace permanently. His Catalan roots, deeply embedded in the soil of his artistic being, could not be weakened, even if at times they threatened to choke and destroy him.

Childhood in Figueres

Salvador Dalí was born on 11 May, 1904 in the small town of Figueres in the north-eastern Spanish province of Catalonia. He was born into a fairly wealthy, influential family. His father, Don Salvador Dalí y Cusi, worked as a notary and was a highly respected figure in the town. A passionate and progressive man, he was proud to declare his atheism and was not shy to label himself a 'Barcelona free-thinker'. The Dalí household, as a result, was often the setting for heated discussion among the prominent townspeople. Separatism was a popular subject for debate, fuelled by an innate Catalan pride in the material and cultural prosperity of the region which had been building steadily since the twelfth century. Barcelona stirred particular feelings of gratification. The city was a colourful, cosmopolitan and individual capital. It had welcomed the Surrealist architectural fantasies of Antoni Gaudi and cultivated the genius of the young Picasso. Don Salvador was fiercely proud of his heritage and was a great lover of music and the arts. He encouraged liberal thinking, yet controlled and supervised it with a powerful, dominant personality. He could be intensely

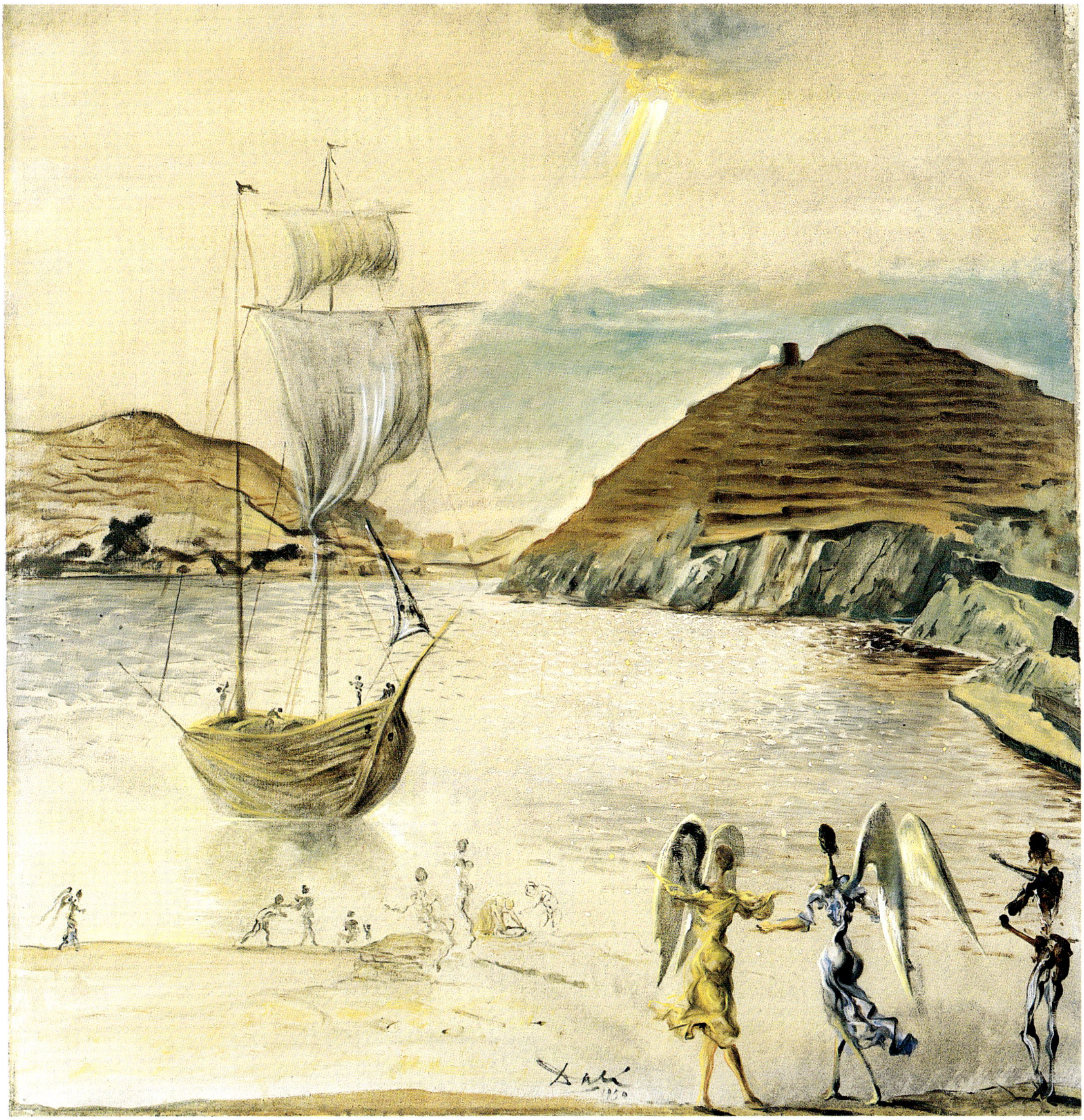

The Arrival (Port Lligat) ***(L'Arivée)*** (Private Collection). Painted in 1950, this canvas, in common with so many of Dalí's works, offers a faithful representation of the landscape of Port Lligat where Gala and Dalí set up house in 1930 and remained throughout their entire lifetime. Oil on canvas. 63 x 63 cm

domineering and his frequent rages were an accepted feature of life in Figueres, reaching legendary stature over the years as his son's fame increased and their ideas became more obviously incongruous.

Dalí's mother, Felipa Domenèch Ferrés, was originally from Barcelona and, in contrast to her husband, she was mild in temperament and a devout Catholic. Her young son, on whom she doted, grew up in a household full of women, including a grandmother, a spinster aunt, a nurse and eventually a younger sister, all of whom gave him

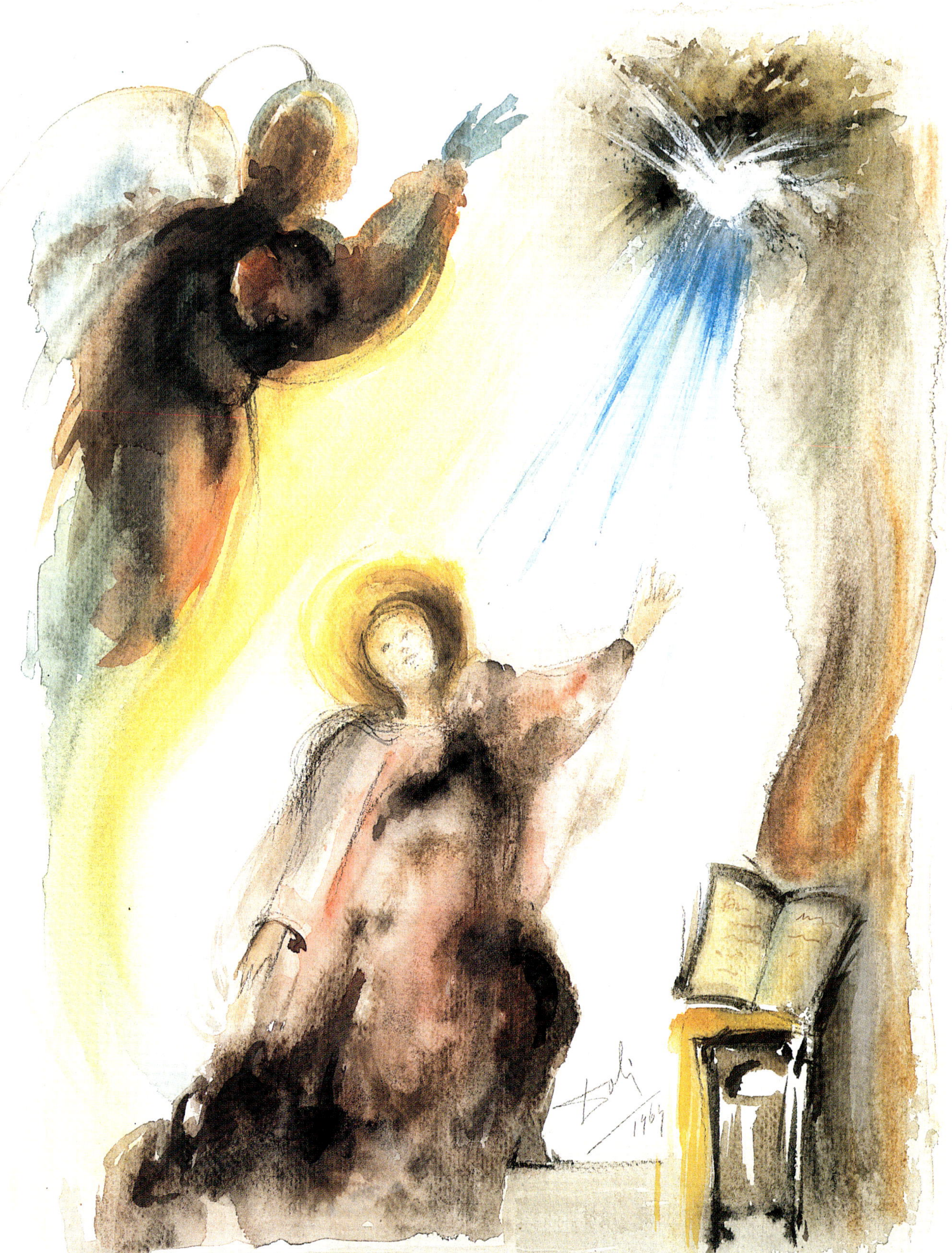

LUKE 1:31

their undivided attention. Maternal over-protection is explained by the fact that the first son of the family, also christened Salvador, died from meningitis at the age of two. Even at this young age, the infant had shown signs of outstanding intelligence and his parents suffered his loss very acutely. The second Salvador Dalí arrived in the world only nine months after the death of his brother and always felt that he was a mere substitute in his parents' affection. He allowed himself to carry this feeling with him well into adulthood and over-indulged his sense of relegated importance openly and frequently, using it as a licence to behave appallingly if the mood so struck him. In his autobiography, *The Secret Life of Salvador Dalí*, which he finished writing at the age of thirty-seven, Dalí still clung to the theory that, from the very outset, he was forced to live in someone else's shadow and that he never recovered from the gruelling effort of fighting for his own identity. His subsequent growth and development into a severe eccentric and immoderate exhibitionist, he believed, was almost entirely justified by the circumstances of his birth:

> *My brother died at the age of seven from an attack of meningitis, three years before I was born. His death plunged my father and mother into the depths of despair; they found consolation only upon my arrival into the world. My brother and I resembled each other like two drops of water ... Like myself he had the unmistakable facial morphology of a genius. He gave signs of alarming precocity ... My brother was probably a first version of myself, but conceived too much in the absolute.*

Dalí's brother was not seven years old when he died and the passage is typical of the fantasies Dalí constructed as attention-seeking devices throughout his entire lifetime. He occupied his fantasy world with great relish even as a very young child, announcing at the age of six that he was going to become a cook and at the age of seven that he wanted to be Napoleon.

> *Aside from being forbidden the kitchen I was allowed to do anything I pleased. I wet my bed until I was eight for the sheer fun of it. I was the absolute monarch of the house. Nothing was good enough for me.*

His ambition grew from this point and he never permitted himself a sense of modesty. He believed that his parents named him Salvador because he had been chosen to save painting from 'the deadly menace of abstract art, academic Surrealism, Dadaism, and any kind of anarchic "ism" whatsoever'.

At the age of six, Dalí sketched his very first drawings. A year later, his father, adhering to his free-thinking principles, enrolled him

The Annunciation Luke 1:31 ***(Annonciation)*** (Private Collection). From 1933, Dalí frequently made use of the *Angelus* as a theme for his work. In the 1950s he produced his most overtly religious paintings and continued to be obsessed with the myths surrounding Catholicism well into later life. This particular painting was produced in 1969. Watercolour and gouache. 45.5 x 33 cm

at the State school in Figueres. He learned little or nothing at this establishment, however. He was conspicuously middle-class and was immediately isolated from the other poorer pupils. He continued to exist in his own reverie, displaying a regular tendency to disruptive and disturbing behaviour. At the end of a year he could neither read nor write. His father then reversed his politically correct policy and decided to send him to a privately run Christian Brothers' school where he would at least have the opportunity to sit school-leaving examinations. Dalí never rose above the standard of an average pupil, which is surprising, given the astounding intelligence of his later prose essays and autobiographical writing. During his school years he remained entirely uninterested, lost in the increasingly bizarre and fertile world of his imagination, taking pride in his difficult nature, revelling in his self-imposed solitude.

A substantial landmark in Dalí's childhood was a lengthy summer visit he made in 1916, at the age of twelve, to the country estate of the Pichot family in order to recuperate from a serious illness. He was first exposed to French Impressionism during this stay and came to admire greatly the works of Degas, Renoir and Manet. Ramon Pichot had earned a respectable level of fame for himself as a painter. He had become friends with Picasso and had exhibited in the Salon d'Automne in Paris. Pichot seems to have been Dalí's first role model as a professional painter. Dalí had already begun to draw and paint energetically and had created a studio for himself in an abandoned laundry-room at the top of the house in Figueres. He received every encouragement from his family, but his father insisted he acquire the baccalaureate and hoped that his son would follow an academic career in art, achieving the position of teacher in an official school. In his journal, Don Salvador wrote that in this way, he 'would have the assurance that [Dalí] would never lack the means of subsistence, while at the same time the door that would enable him to exercise his artist's gifts would not be closed to him'. On seeing Pichot's paintings, Dalí made the decision that he too would become a painter, but not in the scholarly fashion his father intended. The importance of the Pichot family to his future and the deep impression which Ramon Pichot's canvases made on the young Dalí are again recorded in *The Secret Life:*

The systematic juxtaposition of orange and violet produced in me a kind of illusion and sentimental joy like that which I had always experienced in looking at objects through a prism, which edged them with the colours of the rainbow. There happened to be in the dining room a crystal carafe stopper, through which everything became 'impressionistic'. Often I would carry this stopper in my pocket to observe the scene through the crystal and see it 'impressionistically'.

Portrait of Gala (Private Collection). Gala, whose real name was Helena Deluvina Diakonoff, was born in Russia. She met Dalí for the first time in 1929 and became an absolutely crucial part of his life. She was the subject of many of Dalí's paintings and portraits over the years. This one was sketched in crayon in 1941. 65 x 50 cm

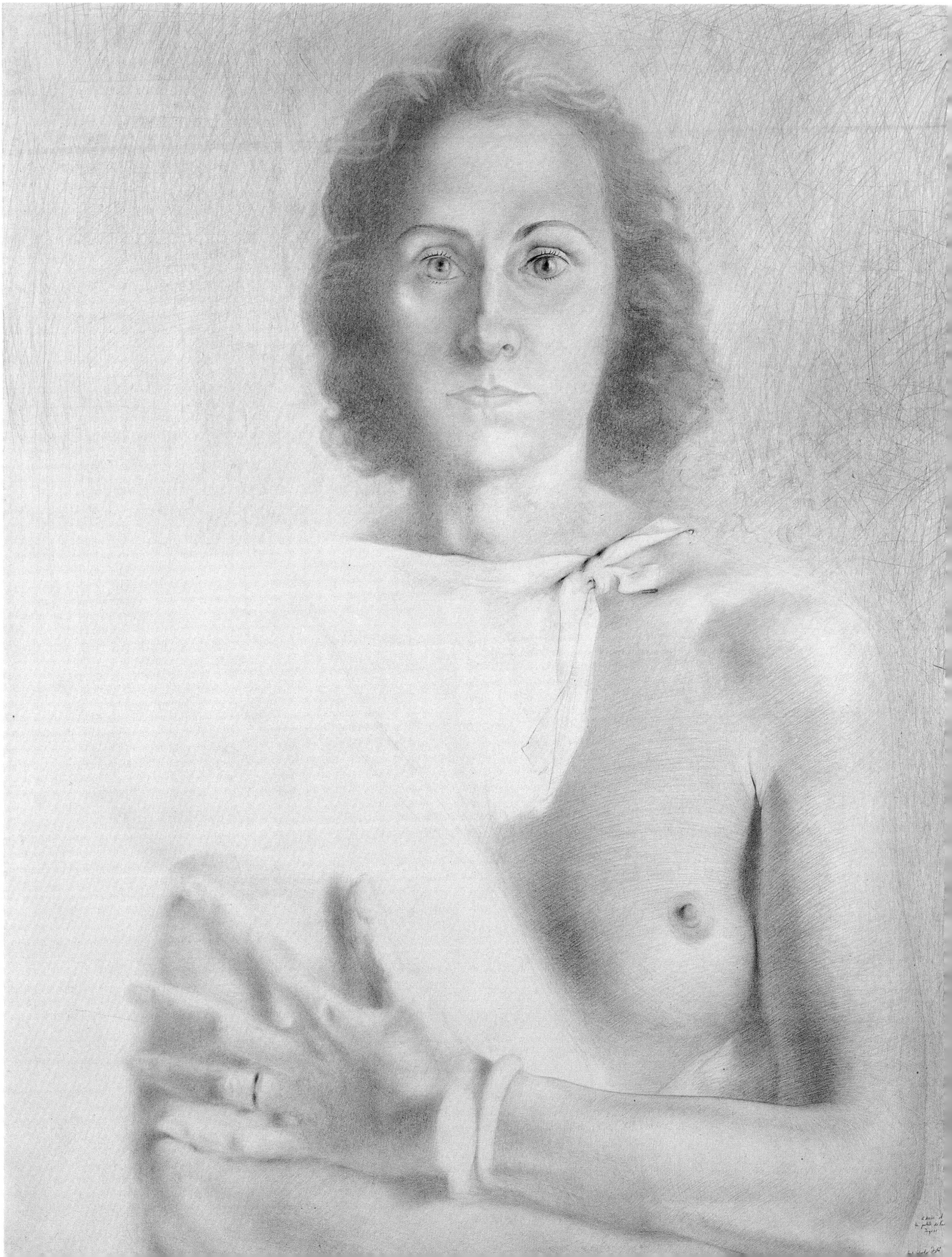

Pichot encouraged Dalí's father to allow his son to attend art classes and he was enrolled at the *Escuela Municipal de Grabado* where he attended a course taught by Professor Juan Nuñez. Nuñez was an excellent academic teacher and the first to help Dalí develop a proper technique by encouraging classical draughtsmanship. He had been awarded the Prix de Rome prize for engraving and Dalí was quick to acknowledge his debt to him in later life. The twelve-year-old pupil was allowed to experiment, but also took particular pleasure in pursuing his own peculiar methods in spite of the instruction offered. On one occasion, when asked to produce a pencil drawing of a beggar with a white curly beard, Dalí produced a black mass of colour and then employed a scraping technique where he wanted the white to be revealed. 'Soon I mastered the operation of bringing out the pulp of the paper in such a way as really to look like a kind of down,' he later wrote. 'On my own I had rediscovered the engraving methods of that magician of painting named Mariano Fortuny, one of the most famous of Spanish colourists.'

It was at this time also that Dalí entered his 'stone period'. He began to paint in thick layers of colour, applying generous daubs of paint to his canvases, creating the impression of having splashed the paint on to the surface. He then stuck stones on to the canvas and painted over them to create a high relief effect. His parents hung his most successful picture of this period on the wall of the dining room – a painting of a large sunset with scarlet clouds represented by stones of different sizes. Periodically these stones would fall off the painting and his father would remark: 'It's nothing – it's just another stone that's dropped from our child's sky!'

By the age of fifteen, Dalí manifested all the characteristics of dandyism and he was already a notorious exhibitionist. His appearance alone demanded the attention of all who encountered him. He wore his hair very long and grew an enormous set of side whiskers to augment his thin, swarthy face. He dressed in a jacket, plus fours and gaiters and always carried a cane. His paintings, at this early stage heavily influenced by Impressionism, were publicly shown for the first time at the theatre in Figueres. They included landscape paintings, scenes of daily life, and a number of paintings of Cadaqués, the little fishing village where his father had been born, which was to be the backdrop for many of the most famous paintings of Dalí's career. The exhibition attracted highly favourable reviews. The newspaper *Emporda Federal* reported that Dalí already possessed 'great artistic talent' leaving little doubt that one day he would be 'a great painter'. By the time he entered the Madrid Academy, Dalí had proved himself an experienced painter, capable of turning his hand to a number of styles and subjects. He had painted over eighty pictures, most of them linked in some way to his family or to the holiday residence they occupied

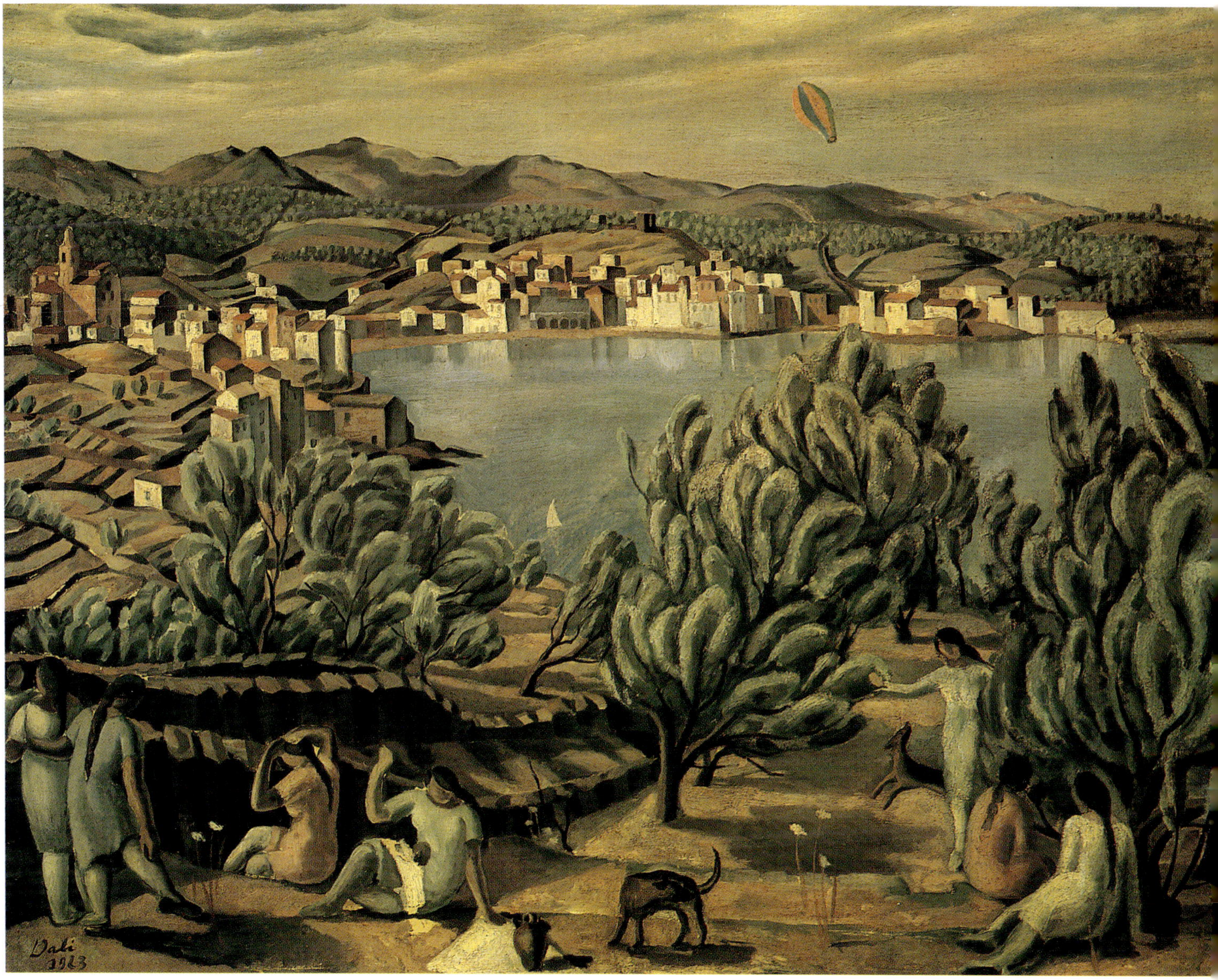

each summer in Cadaqués. His most famous pictures of this period include his *Self-Portrait with the Neck of Raphael*, *Back View of Cadaqués* and *Portrait of the Cellist Ricard Pichot*.

Cadaqués, 1923 (Gala y Salvador Foundation, Figueres). Dalí's early canvases were experimental and he painted in a variety of styles. He was particularly attracted to Cubism in the early years and greatly admired the works of Picasso which he had come across in Parisian art magazines. Oil on canvas. 96.5 x 127 cm

The Madrid Years

Dalí eventually managed to persuade his father to allow him to attend the San Fernando Academy of Art in Madrid, the establishment Picasso had also attended for a brief time. He had the support of Pichot and Professor Nuñez, and the death of his mother from cancer in February, 1921, may also have helped him to convince his father, preoccupied with the loss of his wife, to allow the young Dalí his own independence. He had almost finished his baccalaureate, as Don Salvador

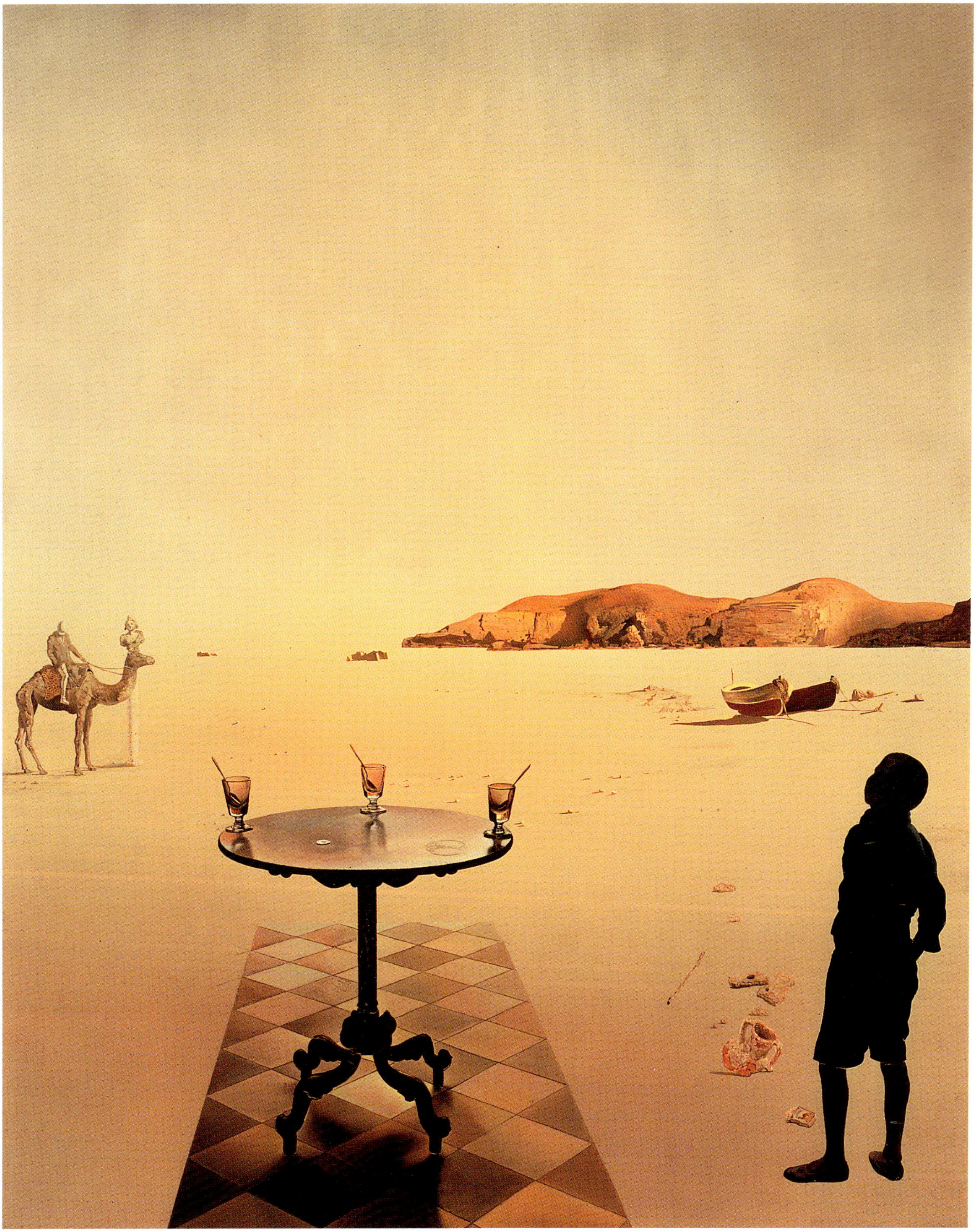

had wanted, and although only seventeen, he was certain of the path he wished to take in life. A diary which he began in October 1919 reveals that two years before he travelled to Madrid, the young Dalí was adamant that he would achieve fame. 'I'll be a genius', he wrote, 'and the world will admire me. Perhaps I'll be despised and misunderstood, but I'll be a genius, a great genius.' This ambition was now compounded by the will to avenge his mother's untimely death. He confessed in *The Secret Life* that her loss was 'the greatest blow I had experienced in my life... With my teeth clenched with weeping, I swore to myself that I would snatch my mother from death and destiny with the swords of light that some day would savagely gleam around my glorious name.'

Dalí entered the Academy in September 1921. Although he felt assured of his artistic ability, he nonetheless experienced some difficulty fulfilling the entrance qualifications. He was required within six days to complete a drawing of a cast of Jacopo Sansovino's *Bacchus*. The examining committee accepted him on the grounds of his outstanding technical ability, making the comment that his work did 'not have the dimensions prescribed by the regulations', but his drawing was 'so perfect' they could not possibly refuse him. Away from home for the first time and removed from the dominating personality of his father, Dalí installed himself in the Residencia de Estudiantes – a *pension* for well-to-do students. He displayed little of the confidence which had so readily manifested itself in his home environment.

He was overcome with shyness during these first few months. Pepin Bello, who later became one of his closest friends at the Residencia, has described Dalí soon after his arrival as 'a person sick with timidity, he was timidity itself'. Yet in the October pages of his diary, Dalí convinced himself that he had 'made great advances along the path of farce and deceit', he had become 'a great actor in the even greater comedy that [was] life' and was 'madly in love' with himself. In reality, however, Dalí confined himself largely to his room and worked there for long hours. While still painting mostly impressionistically, he began to experiment in a whole range of styles, most of which he had read about in *L'Esprit Nouveau*. The journal, published in Paris between 1920 and 1925, introduced Dalí to the Cubist works of Picasso, Braque and Juan Gris. He discovered the pointillist painting of Georges Seurat and the 'highly troubling dream reality' works of the Italian Metaphysical school, including Carlo Carrà and Giorgio de Chirico.

The publication enabled him, above all, to familiarize himself with the most advanced avant-garde art being produced in Europe at that particular time. He also spent long hours in the basement of the Prado museum, studying the works of artists no longer popular enough to be exhibited. Among the paintings which made the deepest

Sun Table ***(Table de Soleil)*****, 1936** (Rotterdam, Boymans van Beuringen Museum). Dalí was well established as a leading Surrealist by the time he painted this panel in oil in 1936. Many of the disparate objects which appear in the picture were features of his life in Cadaqués, including the floor tiles and the café table. The appearance of the camel was prompted by the image on the cigarette packet resting beside the boy's foot. Oil on canvas. 60 x 46 cm

impression on him were those of the fifteenth-century Flemish painter, Hieronymous Bosch. Bosch's pictures were an astounding mixture of Surrealist images and subconscious exploration united with realistically depicted animal and human elements, painted in a rigorously controlled naturalistic style. After his initial experiments with Cubism, Dalí soon turned to a similar form of painting, dominated by the probing of his subconscious and the expression on canvas of his nightmarish, outlandish and profoundly disturbing world of dreams.

Dalí quickly became disillusioned with the standard of instruction he received at the Academy. He had outgrown Impressionism before many of his tutors had even begun to acknowledge its existence. By 1922, half way through his first year of studies, he had moved on to explore divisionism – the technique of painting which had evolved from Impressionism, in which dots of pure, unmixed colour were juxtaposed on a white surface so that from a distance, the viewer was presented with a fusion of intermediate tones. He mastered these new techniques within a matter of days. In a very short space of time he had abandoned the gay splashes of bright colour of his early works and reduced his palette to more muted tones. He painted his first Cubist portraits and still-lifes at this time using only black, white, red and olive green. In some of these works he abandoned all concern for perspective, while in others it became crucial to the geometric structure of his compositions. He painted *Portrait of King Alphonsus, Harlequin, Pierrot and Guitar* and also the more well-known *Cubist Self-Portrait* dating from 1923.

The Residencia's Avant-garde Circle

Dalí had not gone unnoticed at the Academy, but he did not attempt to cultivate a social life until he was well into his second term. His flowing hair and peculiar dress led many of his fellow students to believe he was an actor and he had earned himself the nickname of 'the musician' or 'the Czechoslovak artist'. The Academy had its fair share of revolutionary and anarchical groups who exuded, as Dalí described it, 'the catastrophic miasmas of the post-war period.' Many of the young reactionaries at the Residencia associated themselves with the Paris avant-garde and especially with the movement known as Dadaism, defined by one of its foremost members, André Breton, as follows:

> *Dada devotes itself to nothing, neither to love nor to work ... Dada, only recognizing instinct, condemns explanations* a priori. *According to Dada we cannot keep control over ourselves. We must cease to think about these dogmas: morality and taste.*

Allegory of an American Christmas ***(Allegorie d'un Noël American)*** (Private Collection). Dalí made his very first trip to the United States in 1934 and it inspired a number of canvases with an American theme. An interesting feature here is that Dalí conveyed his impressions of the New World against the background of a Cadaqués landscape. Oil on cardboard. 40.5 x 30.5 cm

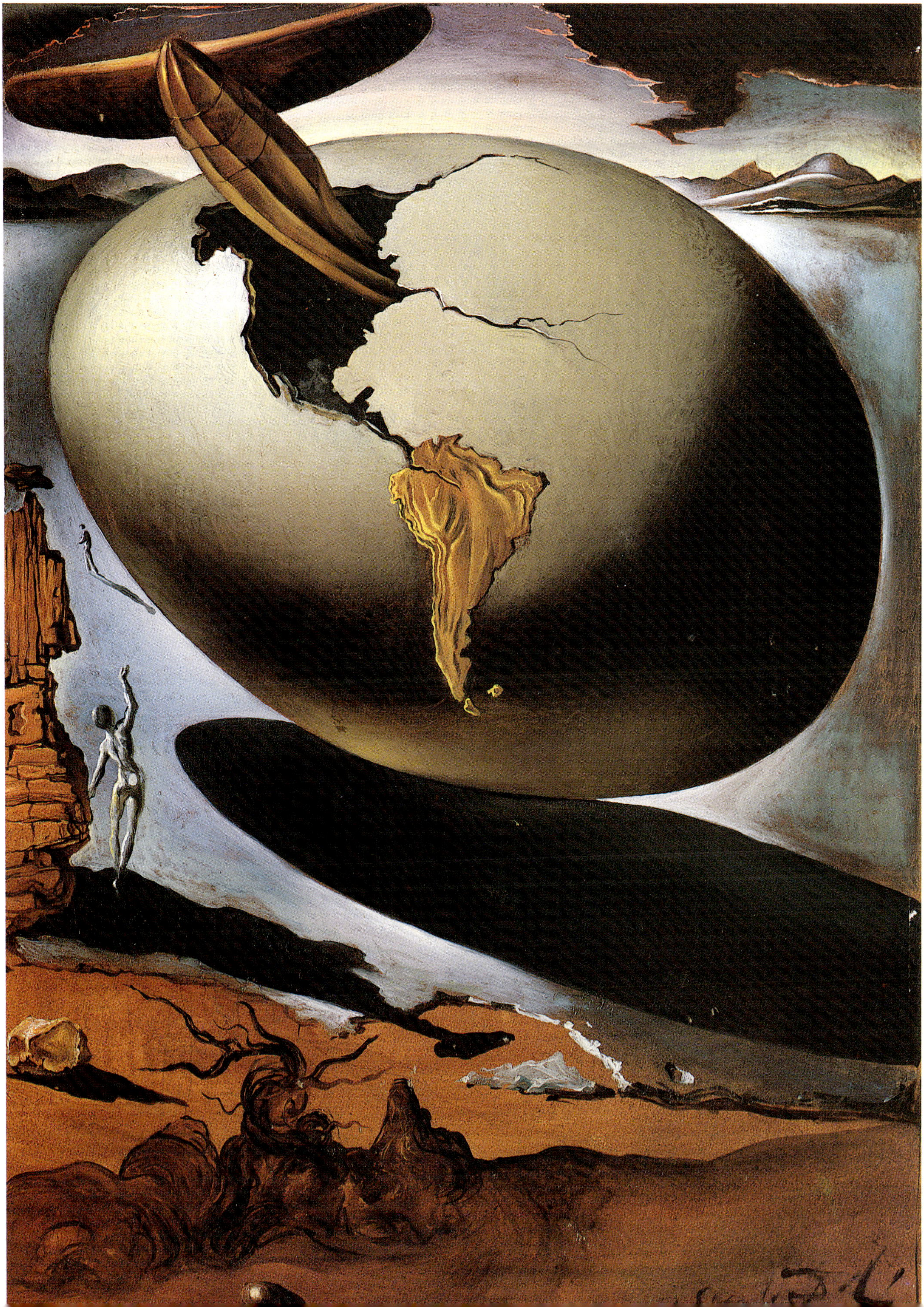

The most avant-garde group of all at the Academy included the young poets Federico Garcia Lorca, Rafael Alberti, Eugenio Montes, and also Luis Buñuel, Pedro Garcias and Pepin Bello. It was Bello who reputedly discovered Dalí and encouraged the group to welcome his participation. He had noticed some of Dalí's Cubist canvases through the open door of his room one morning and excitedly relayed the news to other members of the group. Dalí himself recalls their reaction vividly:

They came all in a group ... and with the snobbishness which they already wore clutched to their hearts, greatly amplifying their admiration, their surprise knew no limits. That I should be a Cubist painter was the last thing they would have thought of! ... I still kept a speculative distance. I wondered what benefit I could derive from them, whether they really had anything to offer me.

The Original Sin *(Le Peché Originel)*, 1941 (Private Collection). One of the many outstanding examples of Dalí's talent for photographic realism which remained a constant feature of his art and was particularly prominent in his religious paintings. Oil on canvas. 81 x 101 cm

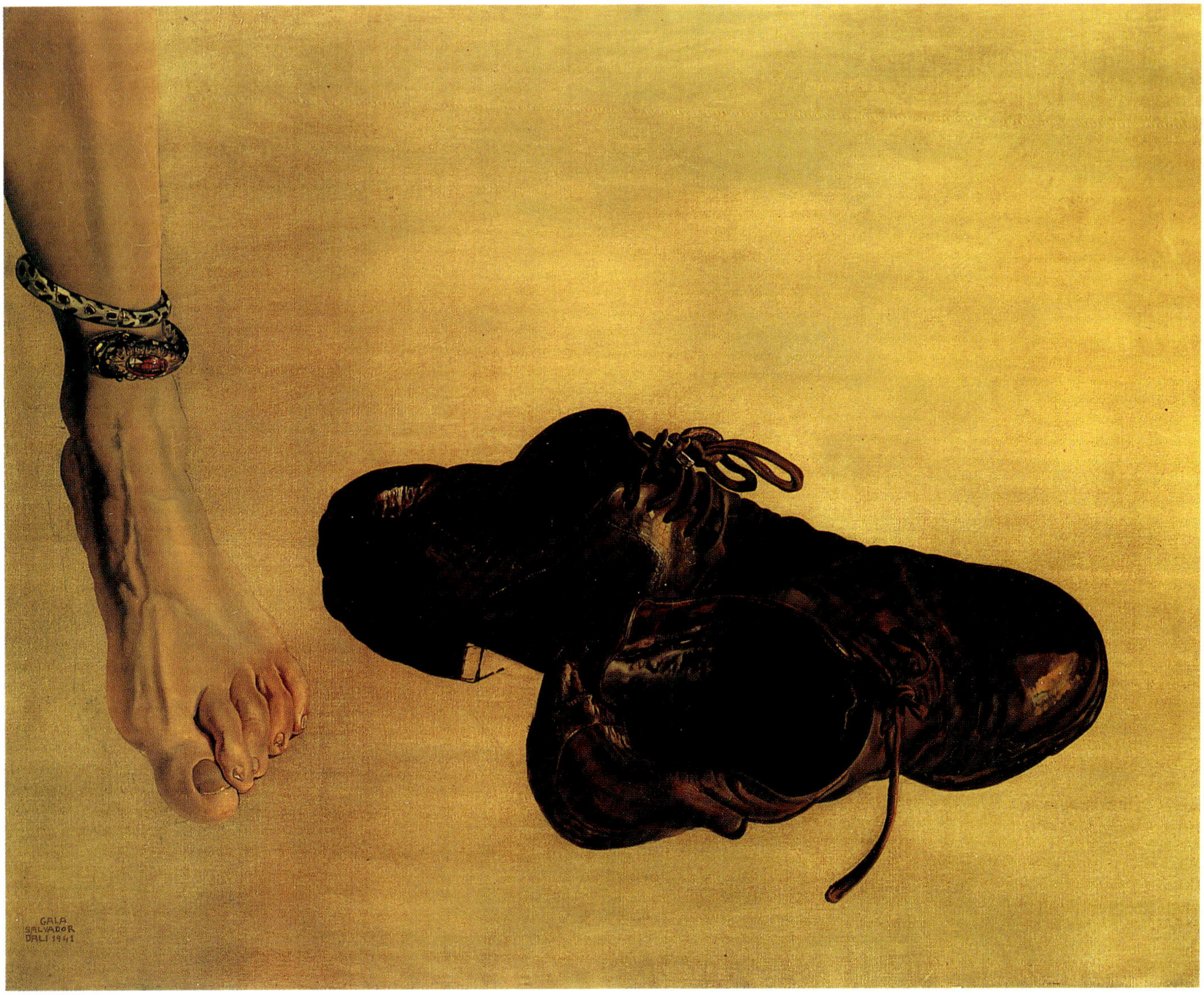

Dalí eventually abandoned his monastic reserve to become one of the leading figures of the group. The months during which these young intellectuals shared their literary and artistic ideas marked one of the most vital stages in the evolution of Dalí's personality and his subsequent art. He now embraced the night life of Madrid and joined the café gatherings of artists and writers. He was introduced for the first time to Sigmund Freud's *The Interpretation of Dreams* and regained for himself the lively spirit and rebelliousness he had possessed while in Figueres. His former eccentricities were not simply tolerated, but admired and applauded. Buñuel, Lorca and Dalí soon formed the inner circle of the group. His two companions were equally protective of him and it was not without a certain amount of jealousy that Buñuel described Lorca as 'brilliant and charming with a visible desire for sartorial elegance ... With his dark, shining eyes, he had a magnetism that few could resist.' Dalí was not among the few and the young poet was to have a powerful influence on him for a good many years to follow.

In October 1923, Dalí was suspended from the San Fernando Academy. He was accused of having incited other students to rebel against the appointment of a man he considered an entirely unsuitable candidate for a senior lecturing position. He was not allowed to resume his studies at the Academy until the Autumn of 1925, but this did not induce any real feelings of anxiety. His painting, he believed, owed little to the tuition he received. During this involuntary sabbatical Dalí divided his time between Madrid and Figueres. In May, he was arrested in his home town for separatist activities and transferred to a prison in Girona where he was forced to spend an entire month. Dalí had no real political sympathies; his only suspect behaviour amounted to a subscription to the French communist newspaper, *L'Humanité*. His imprisonment by the authorities at this time was in retaliation for his father's outspoken opposition to the dictatorial powers of General Primo de Rivera. Dalí viewed the time spent in prison as an incident 'to add a lively colour to the already highly coloured sequence of the anecdotic episodes of my life.' During the summer following his release, which he spent in Cadaqués, he painted and read a great deal. He produced the Cubist canvases *Bouquet of Flowers* and *Port Alguer* and painted numerous portraits of his sister Ana Maria. He also began work on a series of illustrations for a book of poems by Fages de Climent entitled *Les Bruixes de Llers (The Witches of Llers)* which was published at the end of 1924.

Dalí was convinced that the Residencia group were devastated by his absence. 'They were all disoriented, lost and dead of an imaginative famine which I alone was capable of placating', he wrote in *The Secret Life*. 'I was acclaimed, I was looked after, I was coddled. I became their divinity.' He returned to Madrid and enrolled for classes at the Academia Libre where he concentrated largely on nude studies in pencil and charcoal. He also painted portraits of his Residencia friends during 1925, borrowing what he needed from the new styles he had encountered and studied. He painted Luis Buñuel, and a portrait of Garcia Lorca which radiates a startlingly sinister atmosphere. His friendship with the young poet was strengthening daily. The two men shared a passion for aesthetic discovery and formed a firm intellectual bond. Dalí invited Lorca to spend the Easter break at Cadaqués, the first of several visits Lorca made until their friendship, which developed a sexual intimacy Dalí was not prepared to countenance, lost its intensity rather abruptly after the poet's summer visit in 1927. Shortly after his return from holiday in April 1925, Lorca began writing his love-poem *Ode to Salvador Dalí.* It is a hymn of praise to the young artist and to the magical landscape of Cadaqués which Dalí had introduced him to:

O Salvador Dalí, with an olive-smooth voice,
I'll speak of what your person and pictures speak to me.
No praise for your imperfect adolescent brush,
but rather sing of the perfect path of your arrows.

I'll sing your beautiful effects with Catalan lights,
and your love for all that is explicable.
I'll sing your tender, astronomic heart,
your card-game heart, a heart without wounds.

Expulsion and Self-discovery

Dalí was finally expelled from the San Fernando Academy in the autumn of 1926, less than a year after he had re-enrolled. His expulsion was decreed after he declared the board too incompetent to examine his work. The Academy had offered him little of value during his final year; it had not even provided the stimulation of earlier friendships. Buñuel had already departed for Paris to work in the film industry; Lorca had returned to his home in Granada in an attempt to have his play *Mariana Pineda* produced. 'I wanted to be forced to escape all that and come back to Figueres to work for a year,' Dalí wrote, 'after which I would try and convince my father that my studies should be continued in Paris. Once there, with the work that I would bring, I would definitely seize power.' By now, he had a supreme confidence in his artistic output. A new atmospheric realism had entered the paintings *Portrait of the Artist's Father* and *Girl Standing at the Window,* which were completed during the summer of 1925. He was also offered the opportunity of a one-man exhibition at the Dalmau Gallery in Barcelona in November of the same year. Fifteen of his works, many of them painted during the summer,

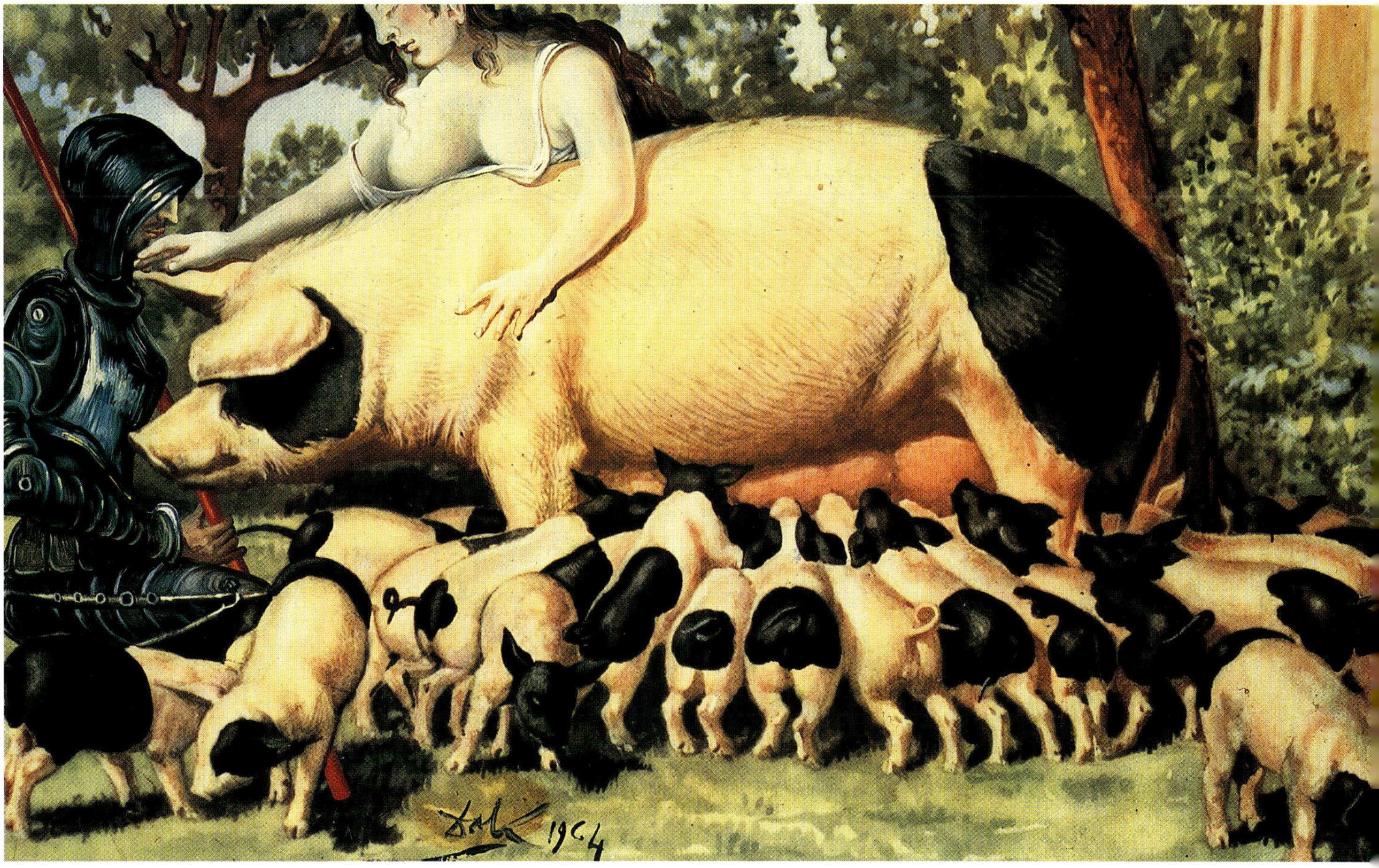

were put on show at the gallery to a highly enthusiastic reception. Dalí wrote of the exhibition in a letter to Lorca:

> *The exhibition has been a complete success, both critically and in terms of sales. I enclose the harshest criticism, the others aren't of any interest because they are so unconditionally enthusiastic.*

His career already launched, he abandoned Madrid and now devoted himself freely to his painting in Figueres. At the age of twenty two, he had achieved an astounding maturity in his art but he was now about to enter a three-year period of artistic isolation which would bear witness to some of the most innovative changes in his work. This was the time of Dalí's transition into Surrealism. He was asked to give a second exhibition at the Dalmau Gallery, and already he had moved towards an even more heightened realism in his art and also introduced a more explicitly mystical quality. Paintings such as *Landscape at Penya-Segats* and *Basket of Bread* contain the essential genetic material of his works to follow. He successfully demonstrated that he had mastered the technique of realism which would be employed again and again in his Surrealist paintings. He was entering the period where his works ceased to be derivative. Salvador Dalí had come into being.

Don Quixote *(Don Quichotte)*, 1964 (Private Collection). In 1956 Dalí was commissioned to illustrate a limited edition of *Don Quixote* and at this time he developed the technique of 'bulletism' - 'realism by quantified spots' caused by exploding the lithographic stones. For this later painting he reverted to a more classical approach with the emphasis on the narrative. Oil on canvas. 28 x 48 cm

CHAPTER 2

The Sovereign of Surrealism

The fact that I myself, at the moment of painting, do not understand my own pictures, does not mean that these pictures have no meaning.

The Conquest of the Irrational

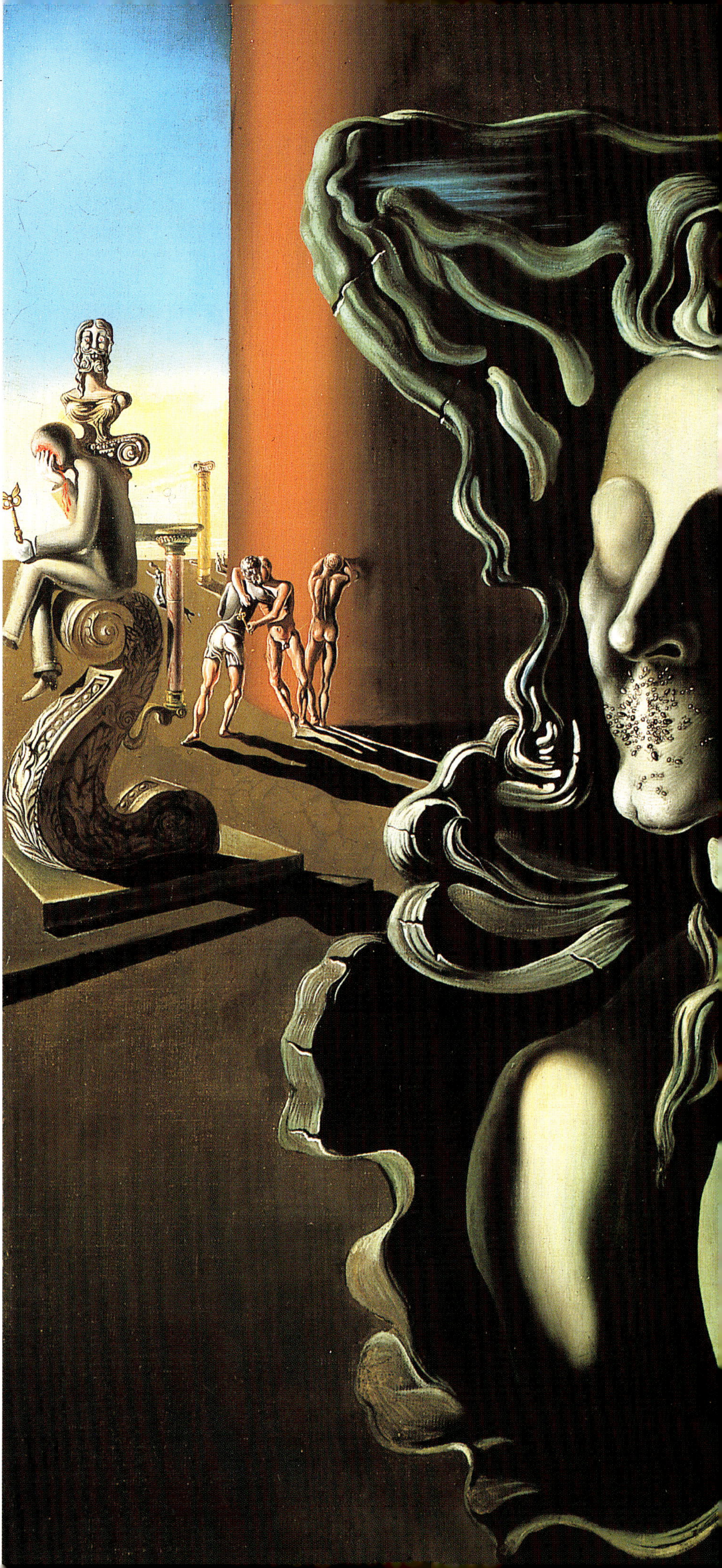

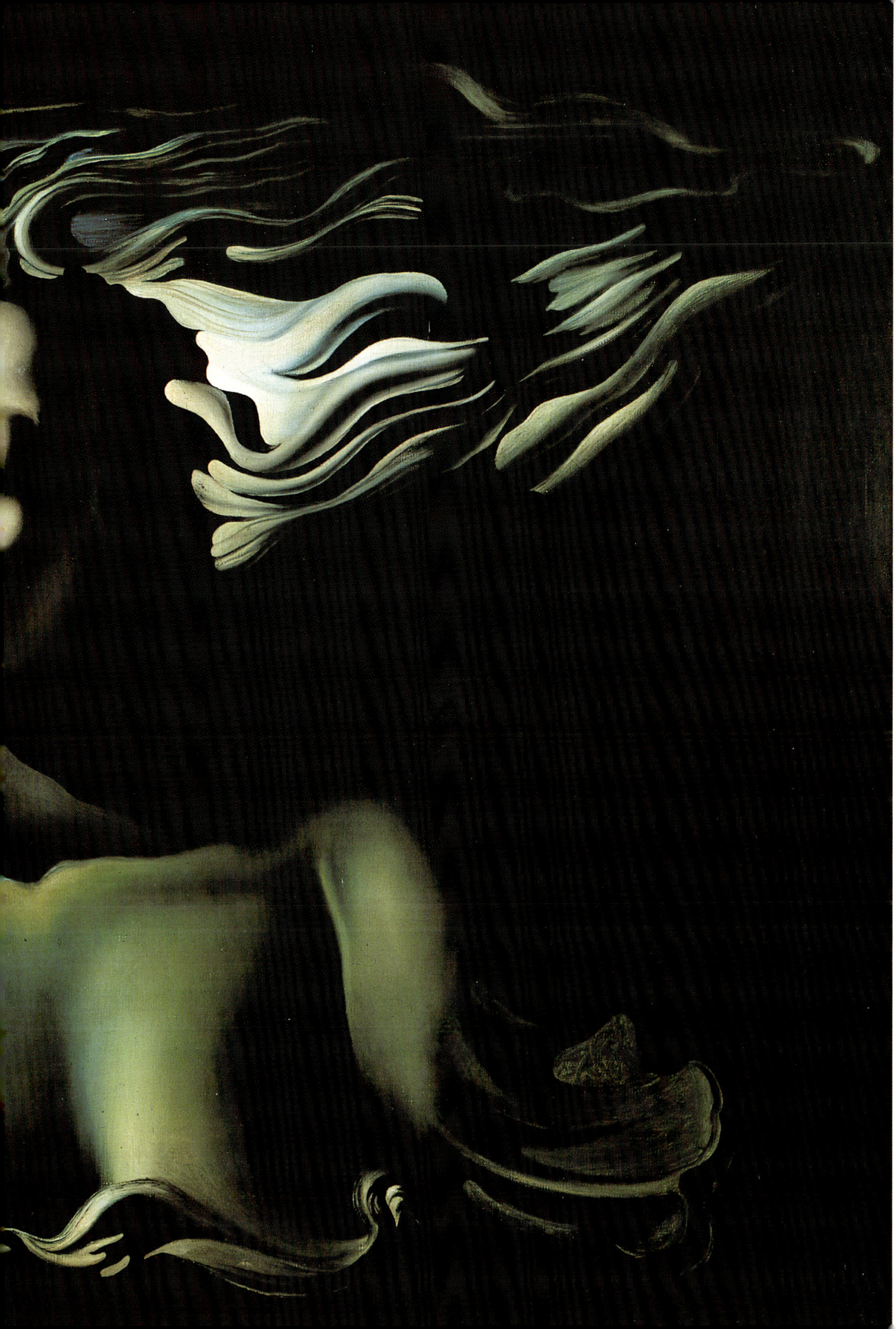

Overleaf:
The Dream *(Le Rêve)*, 1931 (Private Collection, New York). One of Dalí's outstanding early Surrealist paintings, inspired by a monument to Serafi Pitarra which he had seen in Barcelona. Oil on canvas. 96 x 96 cm

Dalí's rapid rise to artistic leadership of the Surrealist movement catapulted him to international fame. Above all other contemporary artists, he became the key figure, contributing to the movement by far the most dynamic and inspired work. His varied talents, demonstrated through the media of art, film and literature were crucial to the ongoing evolution of the Surrealists at a time when the impact of their ideologies had begun to decline materially and the search for a brand new impetus had begun.

The word 'Surrealism' was first used by the poet and playwright Guillaume Apollinaire in 1917, to describe that which was above and beyond reality. The movement grew out of the post-World War I Dadaist organization which set out to challenge all established art forms. The years 1922 to 1924 marked a period of transition from the anarchy and nihilism of Dada to the more constructive and systematized order of Surrealism. The German born painter, Max Ernst, was among those who played a particularly important part in this development. He borrowed from the Italian Metaphysical artist, Giorgio de Chirico, the idea of juxtaposing paradoxical visual images within a single composition, adding to them the preoccupations of his own subconscious. The Surrealists paid special homage also to Freud for his scientific explorations of the human mind and for the emphasis he placed on the significance of dreams as a route to exploring the unconscious. Through Freud, dream-images and hallucinations, the first irrational material of the psyche, achieved the status of legitimate forms of artistic and poetic expression. Surrealism married the intemperance of Dadaism with the expression of spontaneous subconscious thought. Automatism, and specifically automatic drawing, was now an approved method of inner revelation.

By 1924, the Surrealists existed officially as a separate body from Dadaism and were led by the dominant personality of the Parisian avant-garde, André Breton. The original list of group members included such reactionaries as Louis Aragon, Paul Eluard, Robert Desnos, Benjamin Peret, René Char and Luis Buñuel. The magazine *La Révolution Surréaliste,* the 'most shocking review in the world', made its first appearance in December of 1924 and, at the same time, Breton published his *First Manifesto.* He defined Surrealism as follows:

> *Surrealism ... pure psychic automatism, by which an attempt is made to express, either verbally, in writing, or in any other way, the true functioning of thought. The dictation by thought, in the absence of all control by the reason, excluding any aesthetic or moral preoccupation.*
>
> (First Manifesto, *1924*)

Opposite:
The Birth of Liquid Anguish *(La Naissance des Angoisses Liquides)*, 1932 (Private Collection). Dalí's elaborate masturbatory fantasies were the subject of a whole series of very personal canvases painted during the late 1920s through to the mid 1930s. He insisted these pictures were capable of provoking prolonged erotic fantasies. Oil on canvas. 55 x 39 cm

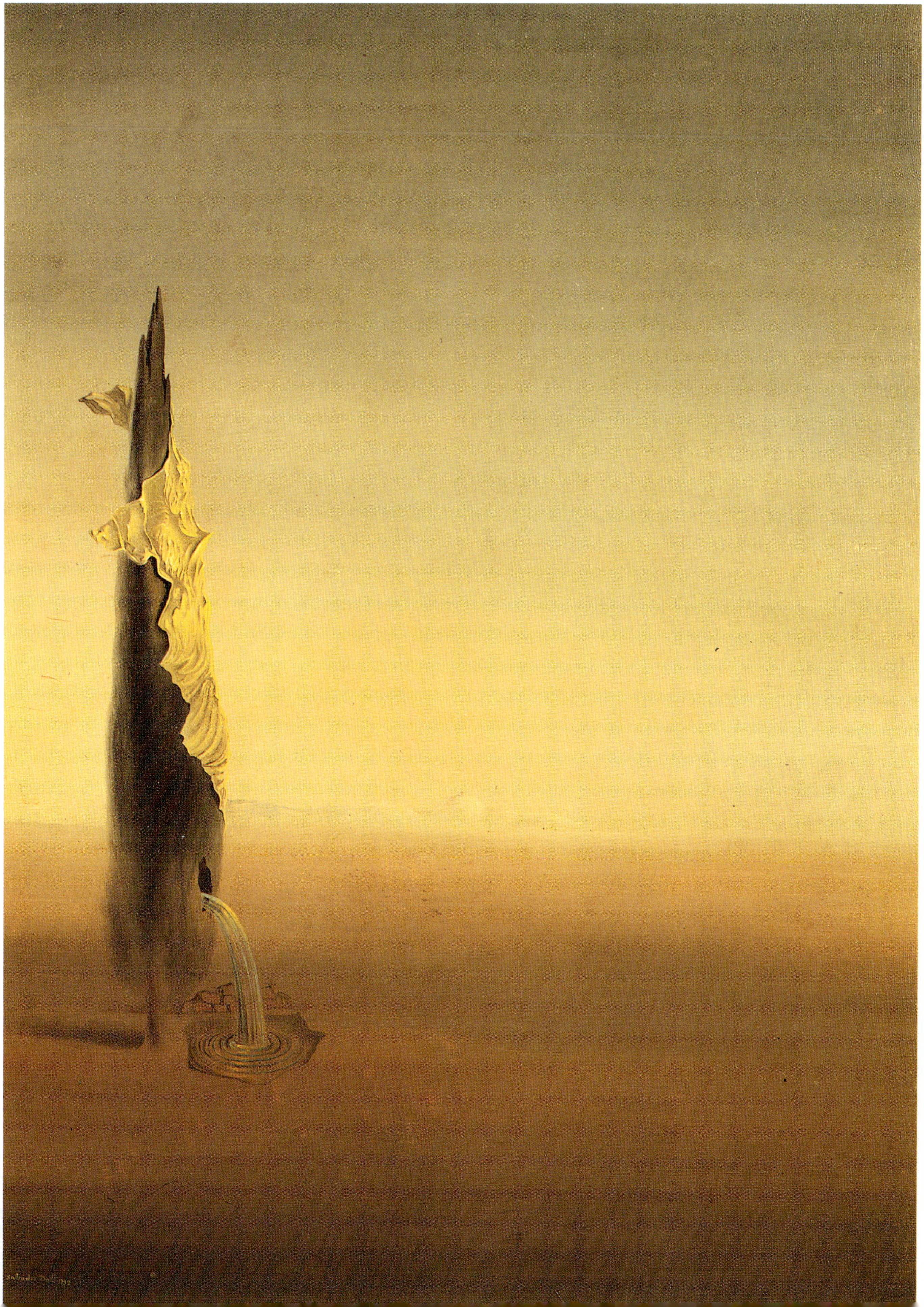

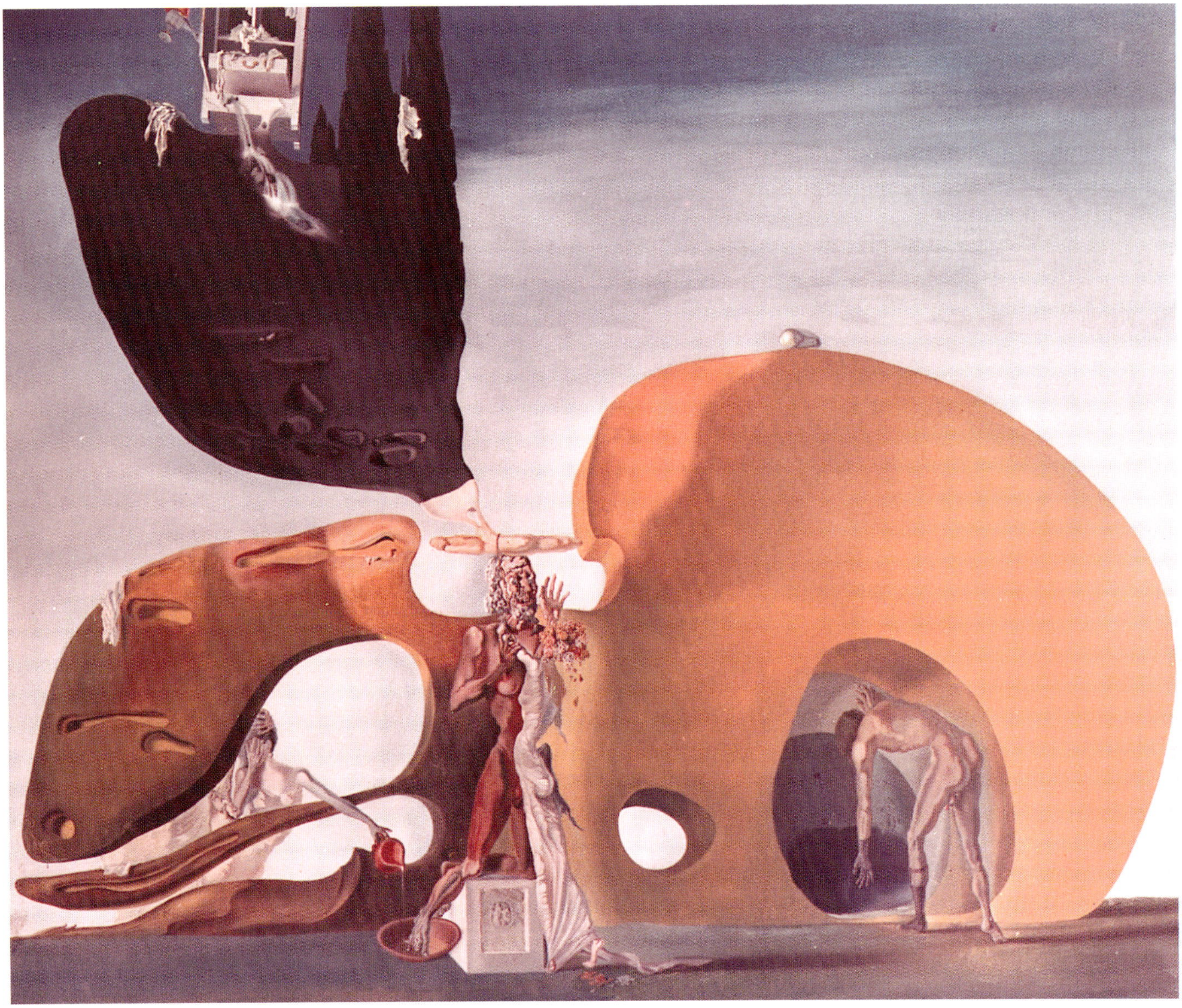

The Birth of Liquid Desires *(La Naissance des Desirs Liquides)*, 1932 (Peggy Guggenheim Museum, Venice). This canvas is another example of Dalí's preoccupation with masturbation. He also wrote about it a great deal at this time in his text entitled *Reverie*. The hermaphrodite who first appeared in *The Old Age of William Tell* is again the central figure of this work. Oil on canvas. 94 x 112 cm

We must remember that the idea of Surrealism is directed merely to the total recovery of our psychic strength by a means which is no more than a vertiginous descent within us, the systematic illumination of hidden places and the progressive clouding of other areas, a perpetual excursion to absolutely forbidden territory.

(Second Manifesto, *1929*)

Dalí's Earliest Contributions to Surrealism

By the time Dalí had finished his studies at the San Fernando Academy in Madrid at the age of twenty-two, he had already established himself as one of the foremost Catalan painters. His second one-man exhibition at the Dalmau Gallery in Barcelona, between December 1926 and

January 1927, attracted a huge amount of critical attention. He appeared to have mastered most modern art styles with the result that a distinct dualism had made itself apparent in his paintings. The exhibition included not only the works which developed further the realism and Romantic symbolism of earlier paintings, but also Cubist and Neo-Cubist works, such as *Composition with Three Figures* and *Neo-Cubist Academy*. Some critics accused the young artist of being too divergent and insincere in his paintings. 'Dalí plays two apparently opposing cards,' wrote Rafael Benet in *La Veu de Catalunya*, 'the traditional card' together with 'the card of audacity'. Several of his new pieces, where the subconscious appeared to take control, puzzled the critics and Dalí was accused of merely drawing attention to himself by wearing a mask of modern art. An important art critic, Sebastià Gasch, wrote in *L'Amic de les Arts* that Dalí had 'allowed himself to be led by fashion', that he had 'plunged himself wildly into the painting of canvases in the style of Picasso's most recent works'. Another critic could see the importance, before following in Vermeer's footsteps, of 'turning a few somersaults in the forecourts of Cubism or Surrealism', but warned that it was important for Dalí 'not to stay out in the forecourt turning somersaults'.

Dalí had not yet properly entered his Surrealist phase, but the second exhibition highlighted a stage where he was beginning to take a more subversive approach and to explore more explicitly the subconscious and irrational in his painting. He had made a study for *Honey is Sweeter than Blood* towards the end of 1926 and this painting, completed long before meeting the Surrealists in Paris in 1929, demonstrated his independent adherence to the tenets of the movement. In the autumn of 1927, Dalí wrote to his friend, the poet Federico Garcia Lorca:

> *I am painting pictures which make me die for joy, I am creating with an absolute naturalness, without the slightest aesthetic concern, I am making things that inspire me with a very profound emotion and I am trying to paint them honestly.*

Honey is Sweeter than Blood was exhibited alongside *Apparatus and Hand* at the Autumn Salon in Barcelona in 1927. It heralded a radical change of direction in Dalí's art and became the key painting in a series of works powerfully influenced by the artist's relationship with Lorca and by the spontaneous impulses of his own subconscious. The picture is geometrically divided into squares by a row of skewer-like objects planted in the sand and draws on the technique of photographic realism characteristic of Vermeer or Velázquez. The fantastic, obsessive images which were to occupy later Surrealist paintings first make their appearance here, including distorted or truncated human forms and the image of the rotting donkey. Lorca and Dalí first used this term at

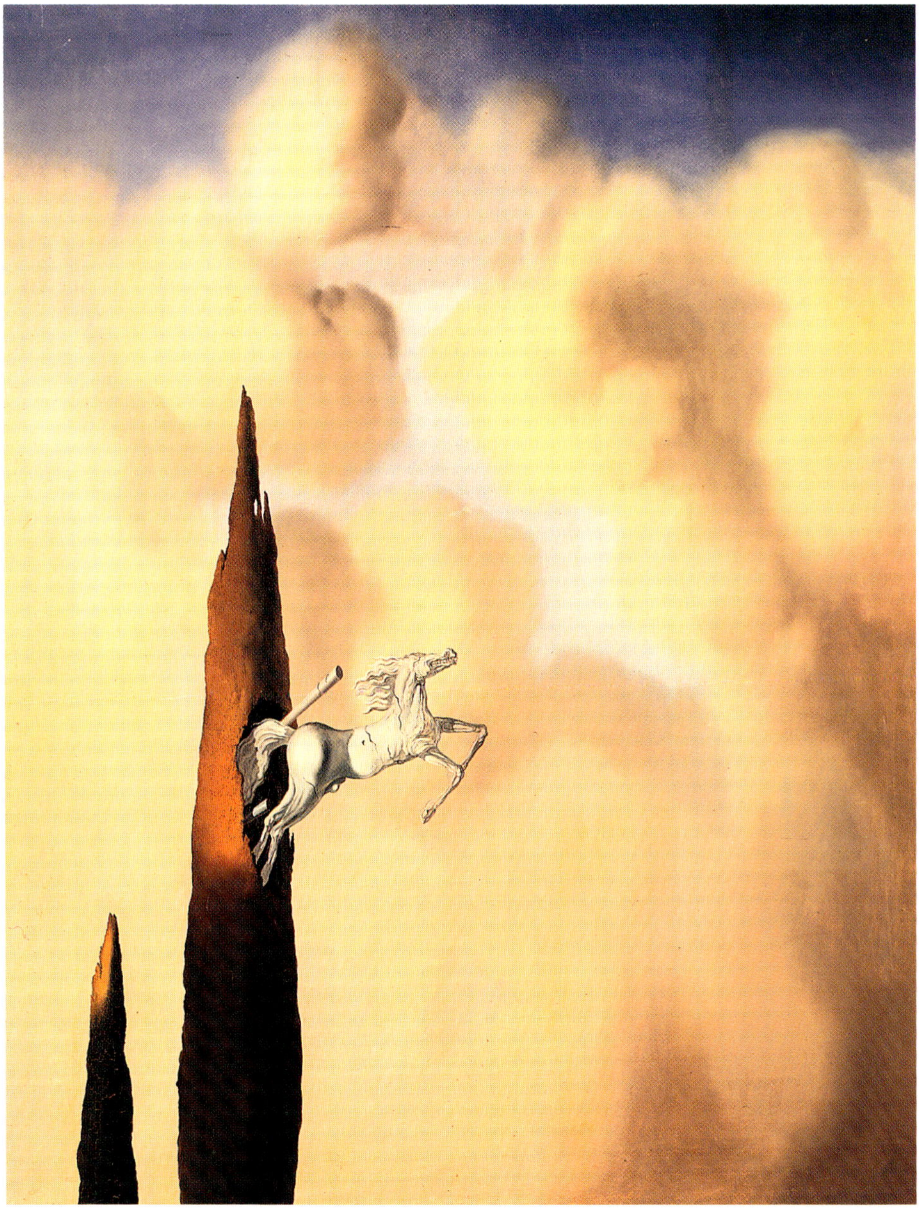

Morning Ossification of the Cypress Tree *(Ossification Matinale du Cypres)*, 1934 (Private Collection). The majority of Dalí's Surrealist canvases are dramatizations of his own obsessions, voluntary hallucinations resulting in snapshots on canvas. He was always eager to depart from established rules, claiming that it was more gratifying than the most absolute given freedom. Oil on canvas. 82 x 66 cm

Opposite:
Apparatus and Hand *(Appareil et Main)*, 1927 (Salvador Dalí Museum, St Petersburg, Florida). This was one of the most important canvases Dalí painted in the year after he was expelled from the San Fernando Academy. It clearly demonstrates that he had developed his own independent style and was slowly piecing together the jigsaw puzzle of his genius. Oil on panel. 62.2 x 47.6 cm

the Madrid Academy to describe conformist philistines. Both of them appear in the painting, their heads severed and lying in the sand next to a decapitated female body. The atmosphere of the picture is extremely turbulent and its precise meaning, like the majority of Dalí's paintings to follow, remains inaccessible where Dalí has not himself shed some light on the interpretation.

Dalí termed his work 'anti-art'; he had decisively moved away from the folkloric and pictorial conventions of Catalan artists and begun a triumphal expedition into uncharted territory. In October 1927 he published an article in *L'Amic de les Arts* entitled 'My Pictures at the Autumn Salon'. His paintings, he argued, were perfectly lucid to those who could look at them with 'pure' eyes – children, the fishermen of Cadaqués, people without preconceived notions of what art should be.

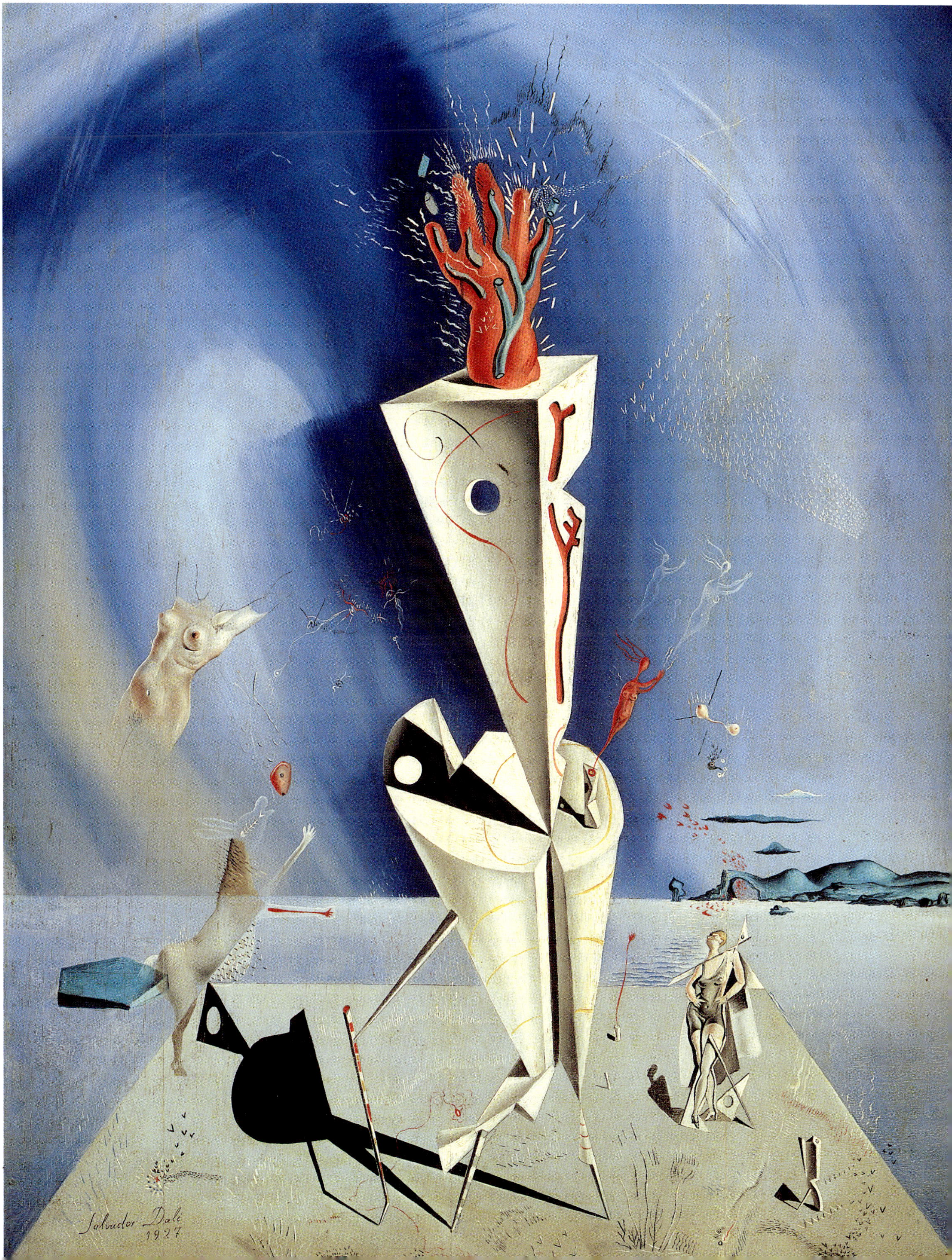
Salvador Dalí
1927

They were only unintelligible to those who had lost the ability to appreciate nature in its simplest form.

The Road to Paris

In spite of the somewhat adverse reaction to Dalí's new style of painting, Catalonian art critics were, in general, of the opinion that he would one day conquer Paris in the same way Picasso had done less than two decades before him. Dalí made his first trip to Paris sometime in the spring of 1926, accompanied by his sister and aunt. He was acutely aware at that time of the need to achieve fame beyond his native Spain, and was desperate to persuade his father to allow him to continue his studies abroad in a city which offered maximum opportunities in all fields of the arts. During his first stay, he records in his autobiography, *The Secret Life of Salvador Dalí,* he managed to visit a number of important places, chief among them the rue de la Boétie where he called on Picasso working in his studio. 'When I arrived at Picasso's on rue de la

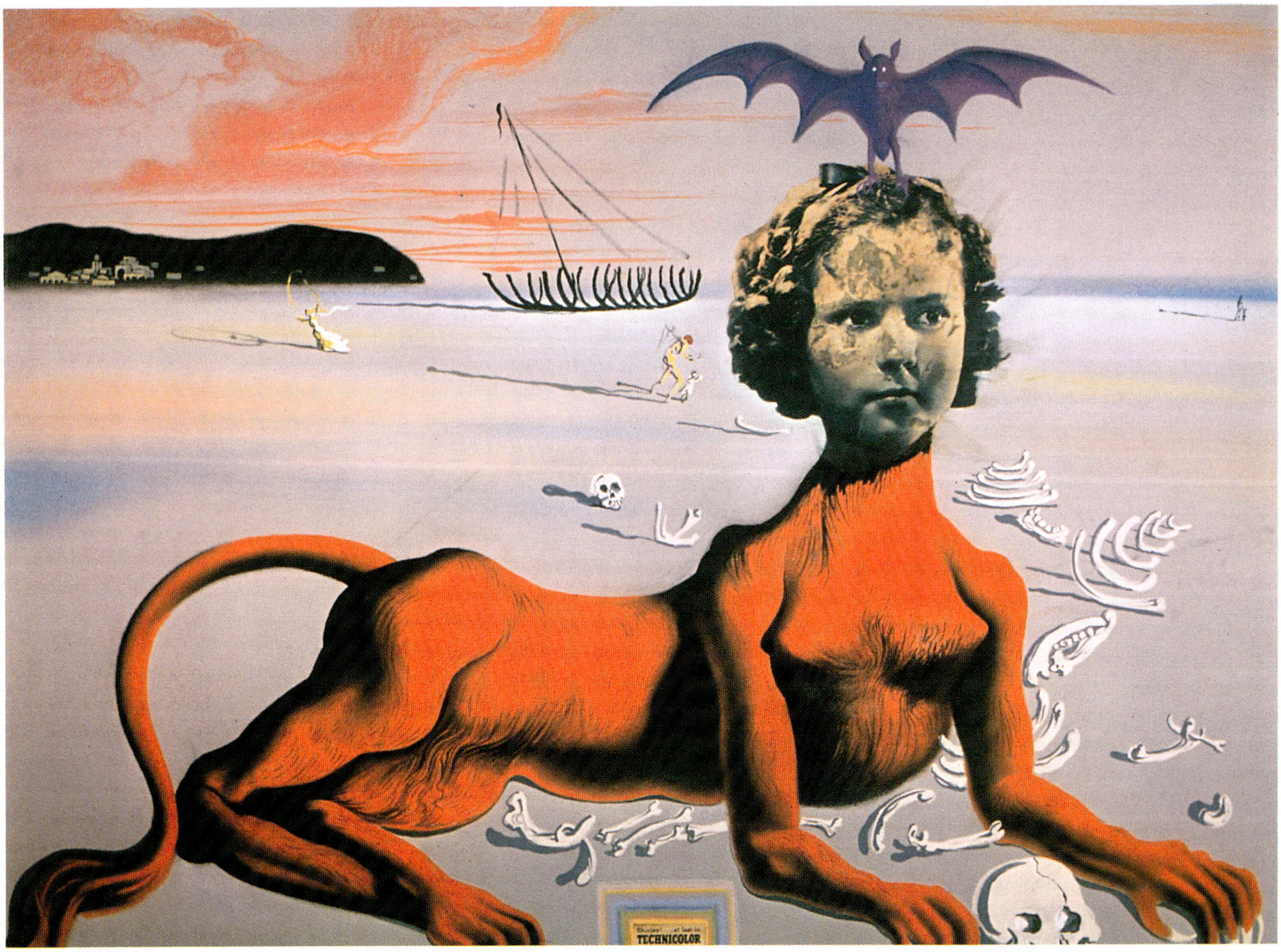

Shirley Temple, 1939 (Museum Boymans van Beuningen, Rotterdam). Dalí never shied away from Hollywood's publicity machine and made several trips there during the course of his career, collaborating on films with Hitchcock and the Marx Brothers. His picture of Shirley Temple, co-titled **The Youngest Sacred Monster of the Cinema in her Time,** combines the media of collage, gouache and pastel. 75 x 100 cm

Boétie,' he later wrote, 'I was as deeply moved and as full of respect as though I were having an audience with the Pope.' Picasso had seen Dalí's first Dalmau exhibition and had greatly admired *Girl Seated Seen From the Rear*, one of the portraits of Dalí's sister Ana Maria. 'I have come to see you', the young artist reputedly told Picasso, 'before visiting the Louvre.' 'Quite right,' Picasso replied in return.

Dalí had also won the admiration of another celebrated artist and fellow Catalonian, Joan Miró. Together with his dealer Pierre Loeb, Miró visited Dalí in Figueres in September 1927. Both men were greatly impressed by the recent canvases *Apparatus and Hand* and *Honey is Sweeter than Blood*. 'The event made quite an impression on my father,' Dalí later recalled, 'and began to put him on the path of consenting to my going to Paris some day to make a start.' Miró wrote to Dalí a few months later telling him that he was 'without doubt, a very gifted man with a brilliant career in prospect, in Paris.' Forced to remain in Figueres for the time being, however, Dalí began to work on a series of controversial Surrealist collages, perhaps in reaction to his confinement, employing gravel and sand and a technique of auto-eroticism. In *L'Ane pourri* (The Putrefied Donkey) he mixed sand and stones of different textures, recalling Picasso's later Cubist pictures, to produce distinct contrasts with the painted areas within a tightly organized framework. Two of these collage canvases, *Figures on a Beach* and *Thumb, Beach, Moon and Decaying Bird*, were refused by the Autumn Salon of 1928 (held at the Sala Parés in Barcelona) because the subject matter was deemed obscene. A written reaction to the latter painting by one private spectator insisted that overt sexual purpose could be 'attributed to the other folded finger, namely testicles, and the masturbatory effect of the hand, and to sharpen the fantasy, the gap between might symbolise rather than represent the female sex.'

Dalí had also published his *Yellow Manifesto* earlier in the year in conjunction with two of Barcelona's avant-garde circle, Lluis Montanyà and Sebastià Gasch, the latter of whom was now converted to Dalí's philosophy of art. The *Manifesto* delivered a scathing attack on the lyrical, sentimental appeal of Catalan artists. It emphasized instead the far more important position of jazz, electric light, the camera, or cinema as modern art forms. The paper provoked huge hostility towards Dalí among Catalan intellectuals, writers and artists, many of whom described the *Manifesto* as 'Futurist crap'. Dalí stood firm in his beliefs; he took a perverse pleasure in the scandals caused by his provocative and free-thinking spirit. He had developed confidence in his role as agitator and totalitarian, characteristics which were to flourish as his career developed further.

In the autumn of 1928, Dalí received a visit from Luis Buñuel, his old friend from the days at the Academy in Madrid. Buñuel was a prominent member of the Surrealist movement in Paris and was keen

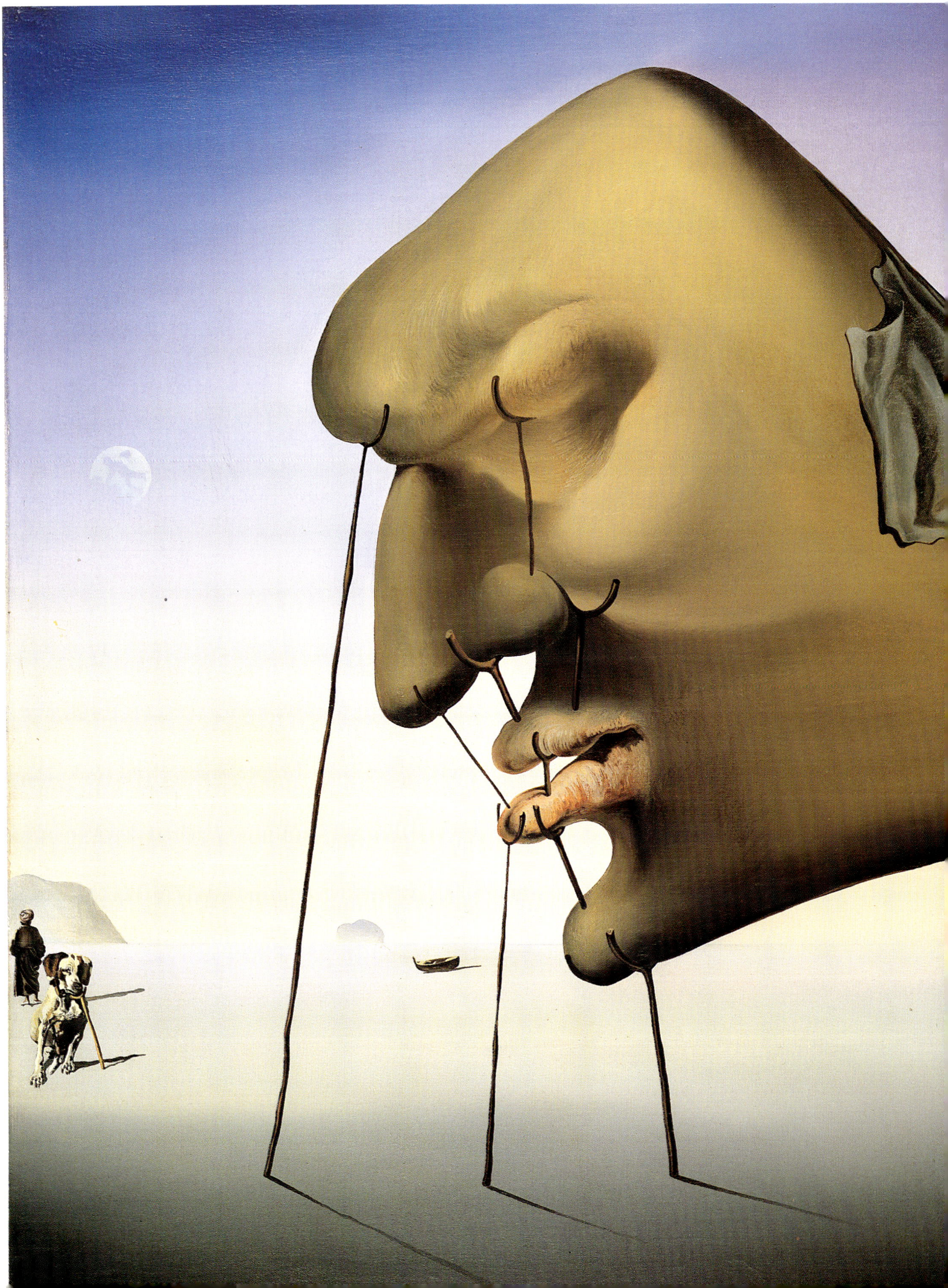

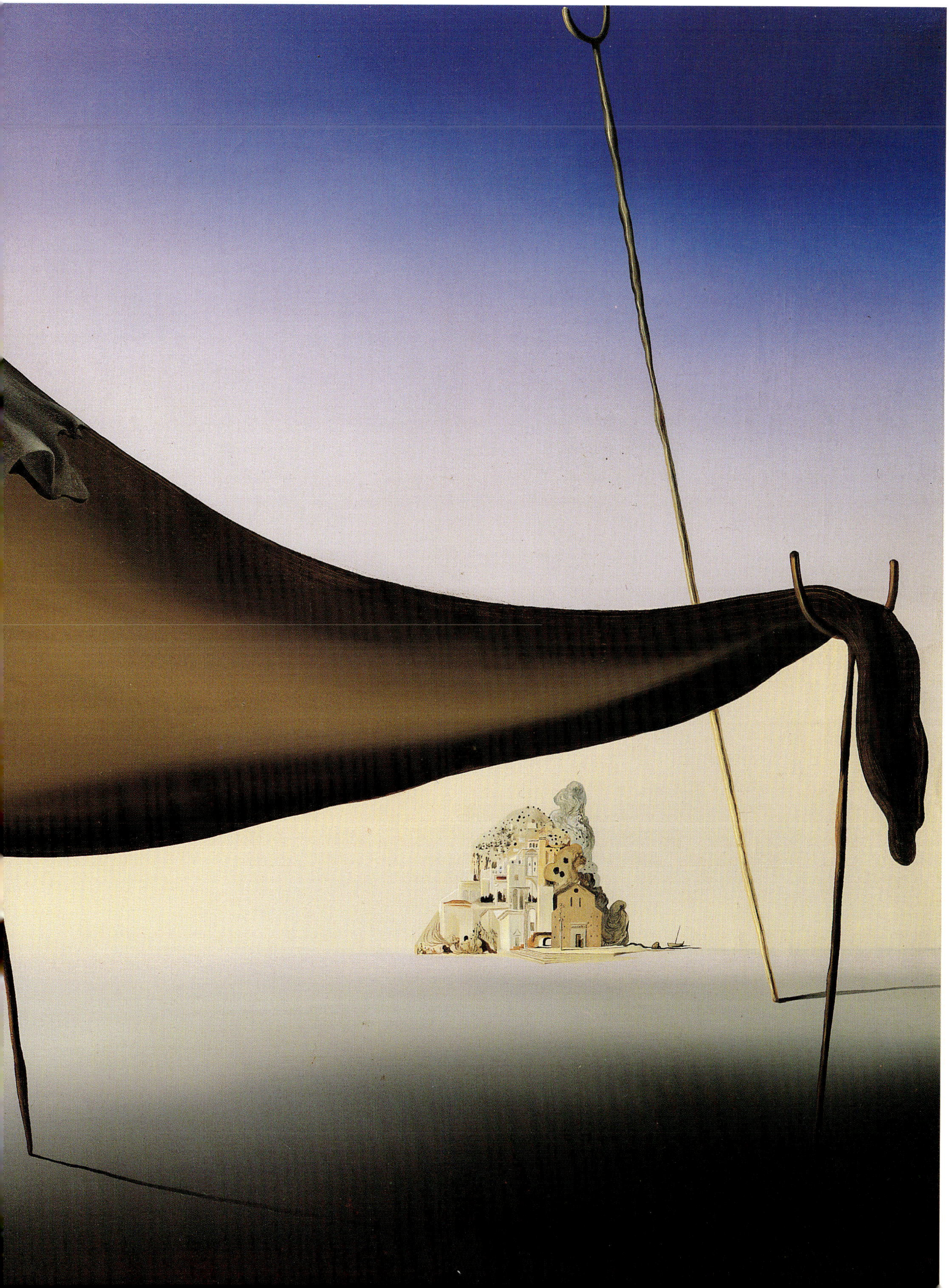

Overleaf:
Slumber (Private Collection). One of Dalí's best-known canvases, painted in 1937, after he had come through perhaps the most anguished period of his art. 'For slumber to be possible,' he explained, 'a whole system of crutches in psychic equilibrium is needed.'
Oil on canvas. 51 x 78 cm

to find a way to combine his knowledge of film with the aesthetics of Surrealism. He had exchanged correspondence with Dalí who had informed him of his keen interest in film and of his desire to collaborate with Buñuel on a cinematographic project. In an article entitled 'La Dada Fotogràfica' (Photographic Fact) which Dalí completed in early 1929, he explained what he believed to be the highly compatible relationship between photography and Surrealism. 'Photographic data ... is still and essentially the safest poetic medium and the most agile process for catching the most delicate osmoses which exist between reality and super-reality.' The two men wrote a screenplay within six days which became not only the first Surrealist film, but also Dalí's ticket of escape to Paris. By April 1929, he had persuaded his father to give him the necessary money to travel to the city to assist in the making of the film. The trip would allow Dalí to meet the Surrealists in person and to establish himself as a bona fide member of the movement.

Un Chien Andalou

Dalí did not take Paris by storm and initially felt 'utterly dejected', having installed himself in a little hotel room where he awaited the attention of acquaintances like Miró and Buñuel. Through Miró, he managed to meet a number of prominent members of the Paris avant-garde, among them René Magritte, Hans Arp and the leading Surrealists Tristan Tzara and Paul Eluard. He also met the Belgian art dealer, Camille Goemans, with whom he signed a contract for his first Paris exhibition in the Autumn of 1929. Dalí felt miserable in the French capital, accustomed as he was 'to being always cared for with the most exaggerated ritual'. He quickly became disillusioned with the social career Miró had planned for him and threw himself into the making of the film he and Buñuel had written together, informing Miró that he preferred to begin his Paris career 'with rotten donkeys. This is the most urgent, the other things will come by themselves.'

The dominant images of the film, death, decay and eroticism, were closely linked to Dalí's painting. Production of *Un Chien Andalou (An Andalusian Dog)* took fifteen days in April 1929 and both Dalí and Buñuel appeared in some of the scenes. They had agreed one simple rule during their collaboration on the film. Neither would tolerate the use of any image or idea that could be considered rational, or governed by psychological or cultural norms. They hoped to achieve a result which would be unprecedented in the history of cinema and were therefore intent on probing the irrational and bombarding the audience with a series of images offering only the ludicrous coherence of a dream. As Buñuel described it: 'We wrote with minds open to the first ideas that came into them and at the same time systematically rejecting

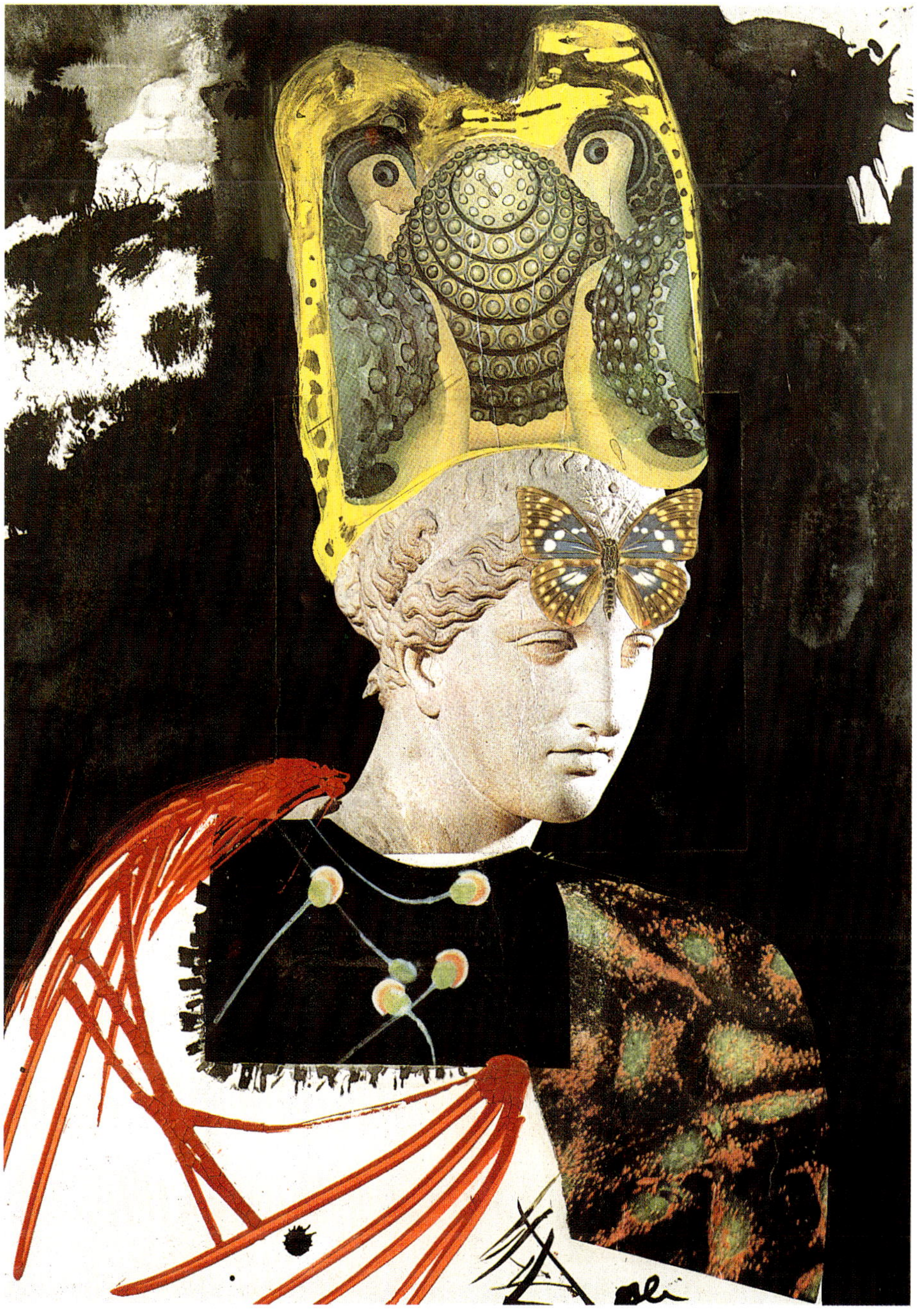

Composition with Greek Head *(Composition à la Tête Grecque)*, 1966 (Private Collection). Dalí first made use of a classical bust in 1933 when he exhibited his *Retrospective Bust of a Woman* at the Pierre Colle Gallery. The entire composition here is centred around the Greek porcelain head, with collage, gouache and ink. 61 x 47 cm

everything that arose from our culture and education.' The first image of the film involved a girl slashing her eye with a razor blade and was followed by a succession of shots, including one of two rotting donkeys lying on grand pianos and a woman's hand crawling with ants, all of which induced a sense of revulsion in the spectator which never diminished during the course of the entire film.

Un Chien Andalou was not publicly shown until October 1929. Dalí had abandoned Paris in May to return to his family's summer residence in Cadaqués. It was at this time that his art underwent the most profound changes, discussed in the chapter to follow, a time when Dalí endowed Surrealism, as André Breton put it, 'with a weapon of the

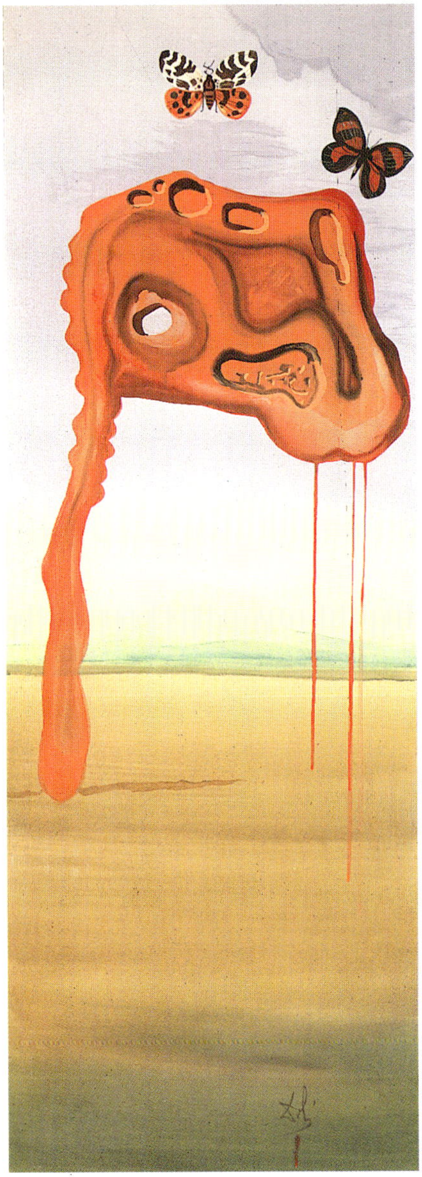

Surrealist Landscape ***(Paysage Surrealist)*****, 1963** (Private Collection). Despite the fact that Dalí officially left the Surrealist movement in 1934, he continued to revert to this style of painting throughout his long career occasionally producing highly abstract works which contrasted sharply with the photographic realism of other canvases. Gouache on wood. 141.5 x 52.5 cm

first calibre by giving it his paranoiac-critical method ... capable of being applied equally to painting, poetry, the cinema, the construction of typical Surrealist objects, fashion, sculpture, the history of art, and even, if necessary, all manner of exegesis'. Upon returning to Paris in the autumn, Dalí's fame was assured. Breton was now convinced of his commitment to the movement and had greatly admired his cinematographic experiment. *Un Chien Andalou* caused a public scandal, producing precisely the effect Dalí had wanted. He had placed himself , as the critic Eugenio Montes put it, 'resolutely beyond the pale of what is called good taste, beyond the pale of the pretty, the agreeable, the epidermal, the frivolous, the French.' Another spectator wrote of the film:

> *The Id had spoken and – through the obsolete medium of the silent film – the spectators had been treated to their first glimpse of the fires of despair and frenzy which were smouldering beneath the complacent post-war world. The picture was received with shouts and boos and, when a pale young man tried to make a speech, hats and sticks were flung at the screen.*

In *The Secret Life*, Dalí recorded his own feelings on the film's impact:

> *Our film ruined in a single evening ten years of pseudo-intellectual post-war advance-guardism. That foul thing which is figuratively called abstract art fell at our feet, wounded to the death, never to rise again ... There was no longer room in Europe for the little maniacal lozenges of Monsieur Mondrian.*

By the autumn of 1929, Paris had become the centre stage of Dalí's world. Having now officially joined the Surrealist movement, he was to spend a good deal of his time in Paris over the next six years, punctuated by lengthy visits to his precious Catalonia. He immersed himself in Surrealist activities, becoming passionately involved in lectures, café meetings and regular evening sessions at the home of André Breton. The movement's leader dedicated a copy of his *Second Manifesto* to Dalí with the following words:

> To Salvador Dalí
> *whose name is synonymous for me with revelation in the sense of dazzling and overwhelming that I have always understood the word to mean, with my affection, my confidence and the absolutely boundless hopes he inspires in me.*

The intense period of devotion to the Surrealist movement ended with Dalí's expulsion in 1934, although he continued to exhibit with

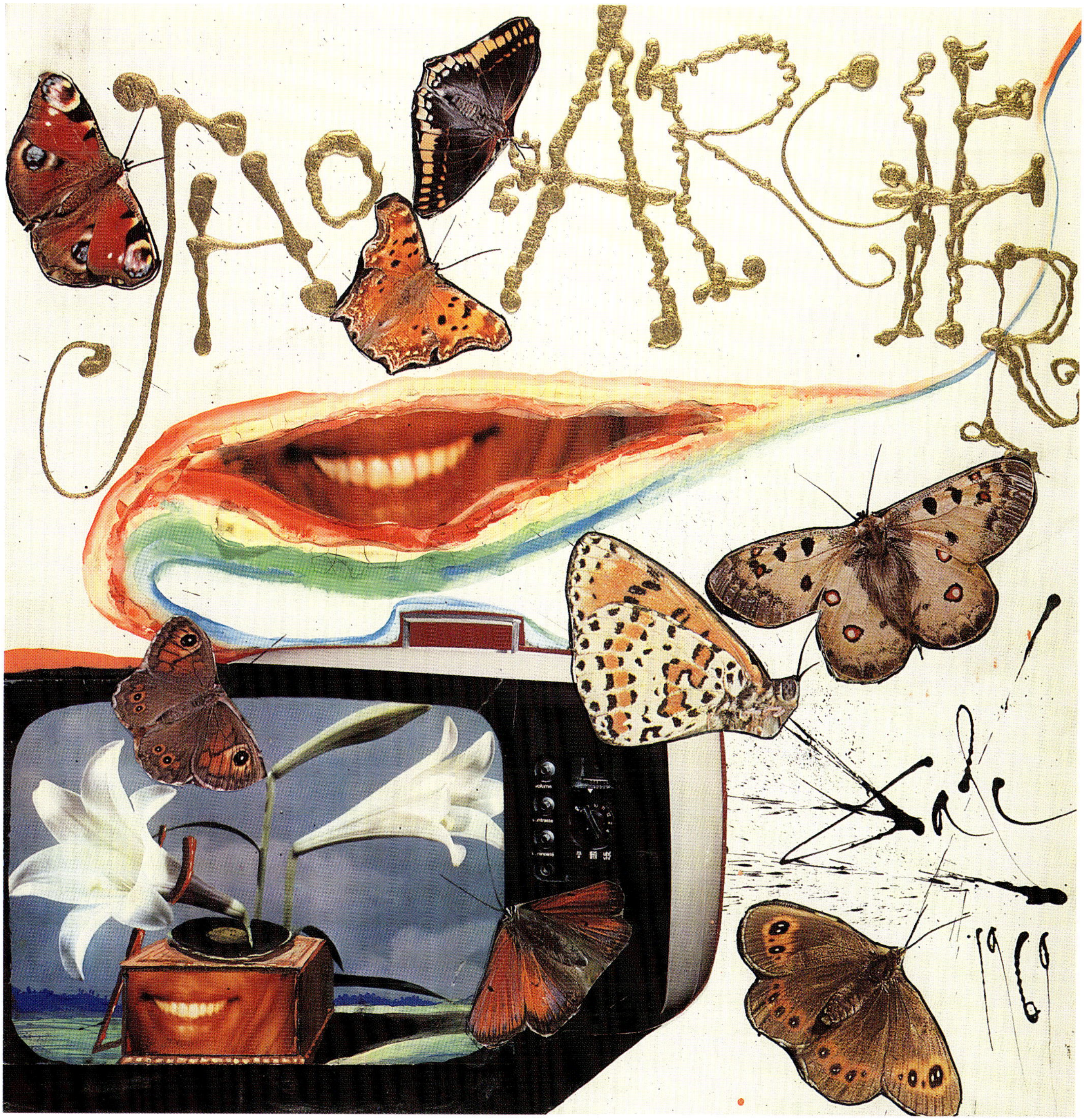

the Surrealists for quite a number of years after this event. The succession of styles he went on to adopt and develop, whether realistic, abstract, Neo-Cubist, paranoiac-critical, historical, stereoscopic, or mystical, could not be accommodated within the movement. He had quickly outgrown the officialdom of Breton and needed to promote himself independently. Above everything else, Dalí was driven to exercise a lack of control in his art. He could no longer align himself with hard-line Surrealists who ultimately considered this an alarming risk.

Study for a Record Sleeve ***(Manquette de Couverture de Disque)*****, 1969** (Private Collection). At the age of sixty-five, Dalí still exuded a startling creative energy. Even at this stage of his career, he sought a new medium, and found it in the music industry. There is no mention however, of the album sleeve ever being used for commercial purposes. 31 x 31 cm

CHAPTER 3

Gala-Dalí and Port Lligat

The most important things that can happen to any painter in our time are these:
1. To be Spanish.
2. To be called Gala Salvador Dalí.

Diary of a Genius

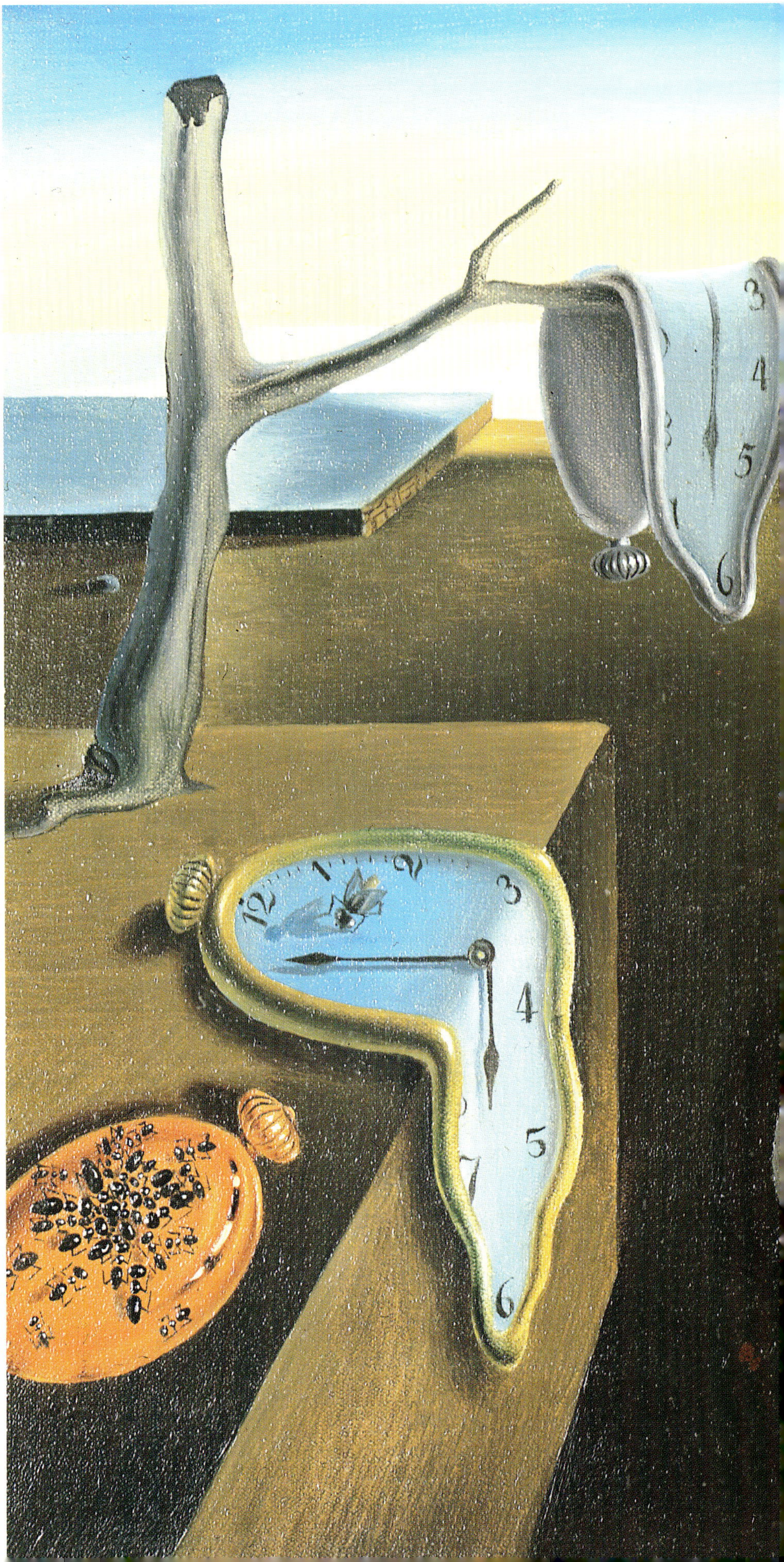

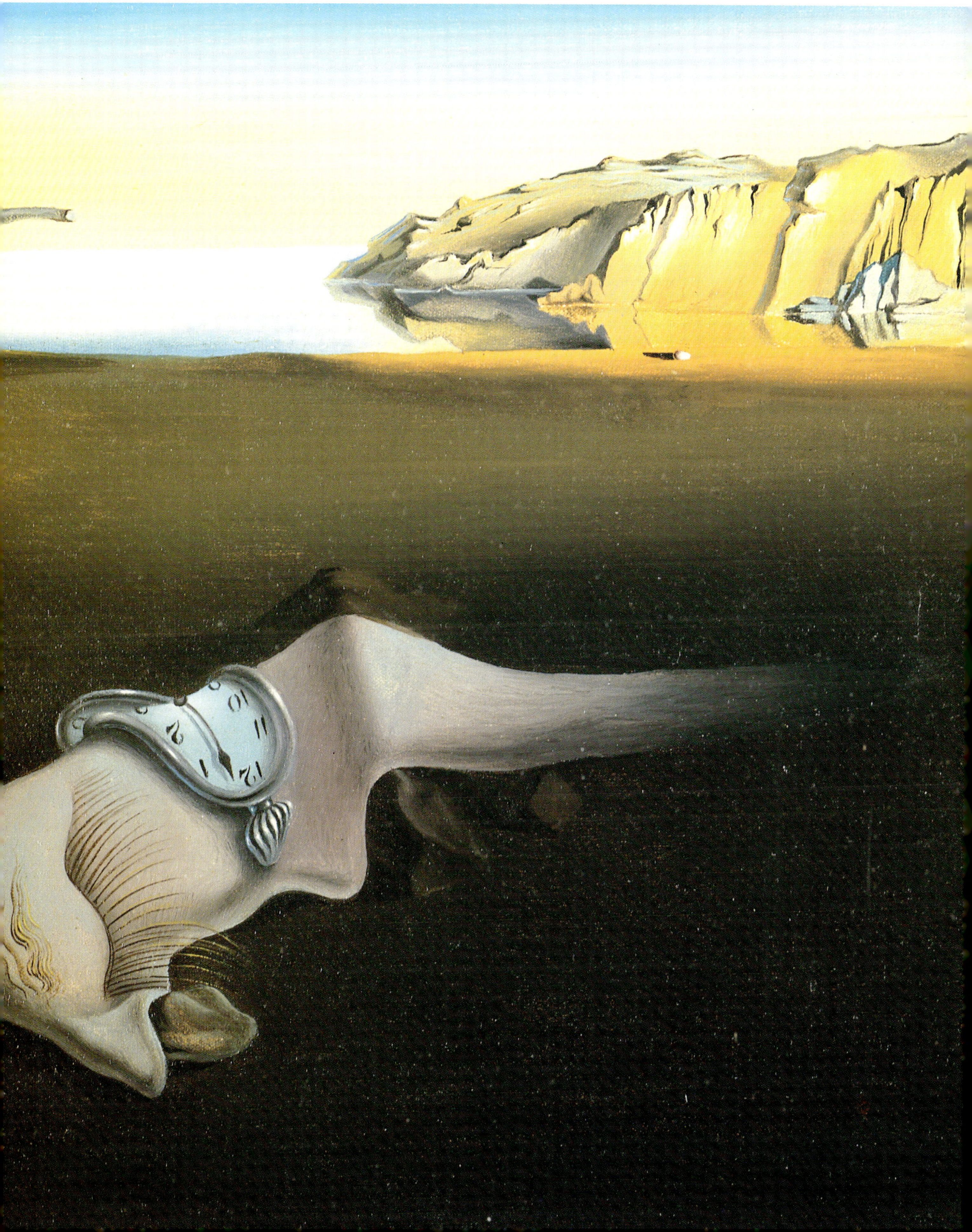

Overleaf:
The Persistence of Memory – Soft Watches *(Persistence de la Mémoire)*, 1931 (Museum of Modern Art, New York). Dalí has attributed his inspiration for this painting to a camembert cheese eaten on the evening he began the work. 'Just as I am astonished that a bank clerk never eats a cheque,' he wrote later, 'so too am I astonished that no painter before me ever thought of painting a soft watch.' Oil on canvas. 24 x 33 cm

Opposite:
The Enigma of Desire – Detail *(L'énigme du Desir – Ma mère, ma mère, ma mère)*, 1929 (Private Collection). Identical imagery appears in many of the canvases painted between 1929 and 1931. This larger painting includes the familiar head with the large nose, the yellow lion, the crawling ants and the grasshopper, all obsessive expressions of Dalí's sexual anxiety. Oil on canvas. 110 x 150 cm

Dalí has never considered himself a madman, but there were certainly periods in his life when he teetered on the brink of insanity. At the best of times, he maintained what might be described as a delicate relationship with normality. A tenuous, as opposed to a firm, grasp was necessary in order for him to evolve as an apostle of the 'concrete irrational' and Dalí indulged his eccentricities to the point where he ultimately welcomed the personal loss of control.

Paranoia and Salvation

He had reached such a crisis of mental equilibrium upon his return from Paris in May 1929. Having failed to achieve notoriety during his time abroad, he had returned to Cadaqués, but had not yet abandoned his ambition to conquer Paris. These months were to be the last Dalí would spend with his family at their summer residence. He abruptly came to the realization that his ongoing success would entail a decisive financial and emotional break from his father, who still continued to dominate his life and criticize his son's extravagances. Over the summer period Dalí began to show signs of a severe nervous breakdown. He would frequently burst into fits of manic laughter, accompanied by painful spasms, at which his father would simply remark: 'What's going on? That child laughing again.'

His art soon began to reflect the hysterical tension within him. Up to this point, Dalí's paintings had been moving simultaneously towards anti-aesthetic and abstract themes. He now felt 'assailed by his childhood' and began to paint profoundly disturbing *trompe l'oeil* pictures of his dreams, much smaller than any of his previous canvases, full of scatology and 'erotic delirium', executed in minute photographic detail. All of the pictures were painted in oil with some added collage. They were produced on panels of olive wood, made by a carpenter in Cadaqués whose services the artist continued to make use of for the next thirty years. Dalí's sister, Ana Maria, was especially worried for his mental health at this juncture. The fact that he had begun obsessively to pursue images which inspired him with horror was of particular concern, and she attributed his developing neurosis to the poisonous influence of the Surrealists:

> *The pictures which he painted were horribly hallucinatory. He designed real nightmares on his canvases and the disturbing figures were like torture, seemingly trying to explain the inexplicable – things which, as in dreams, seem to have some meaning when seen but then leave only the memory of hallucination.*

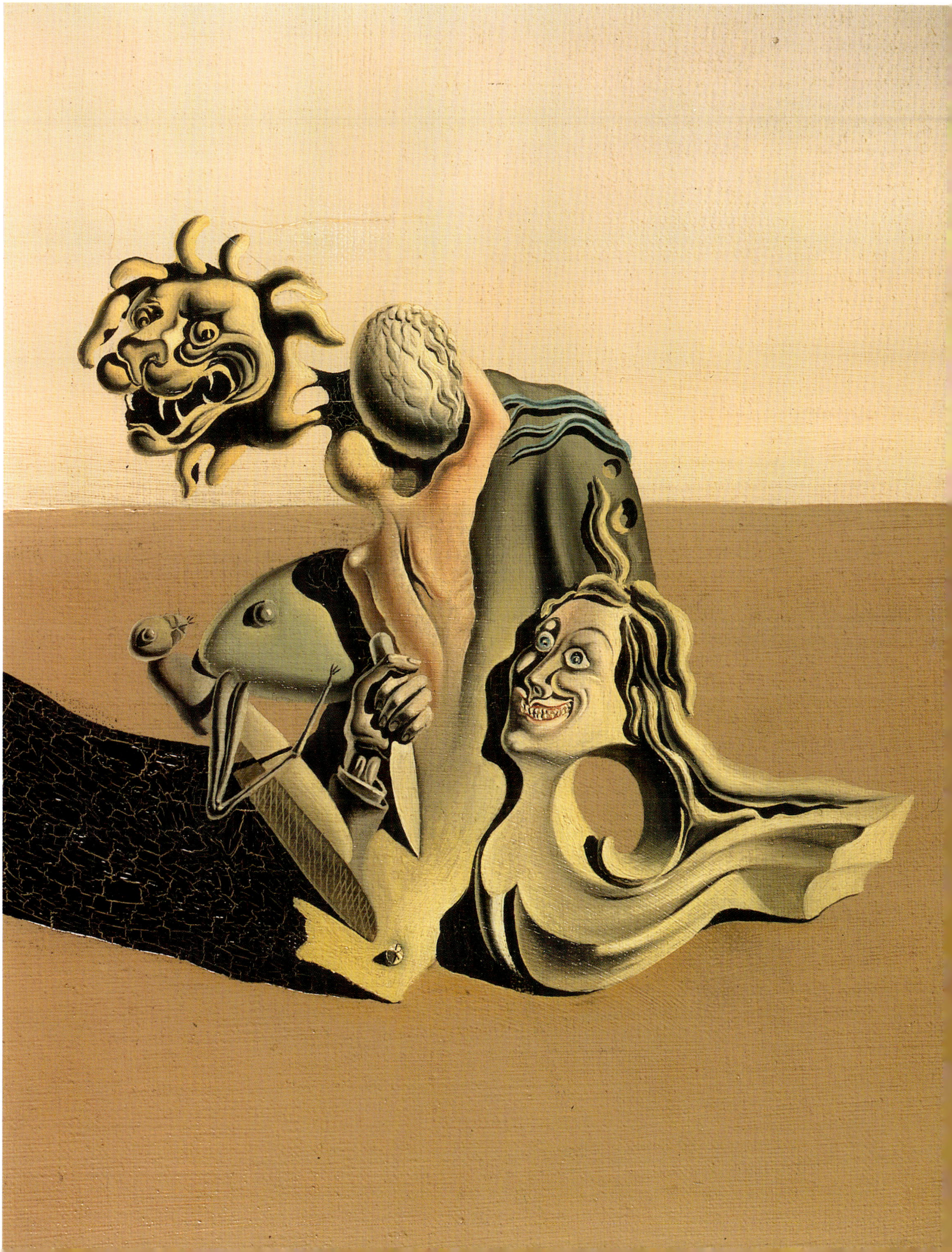

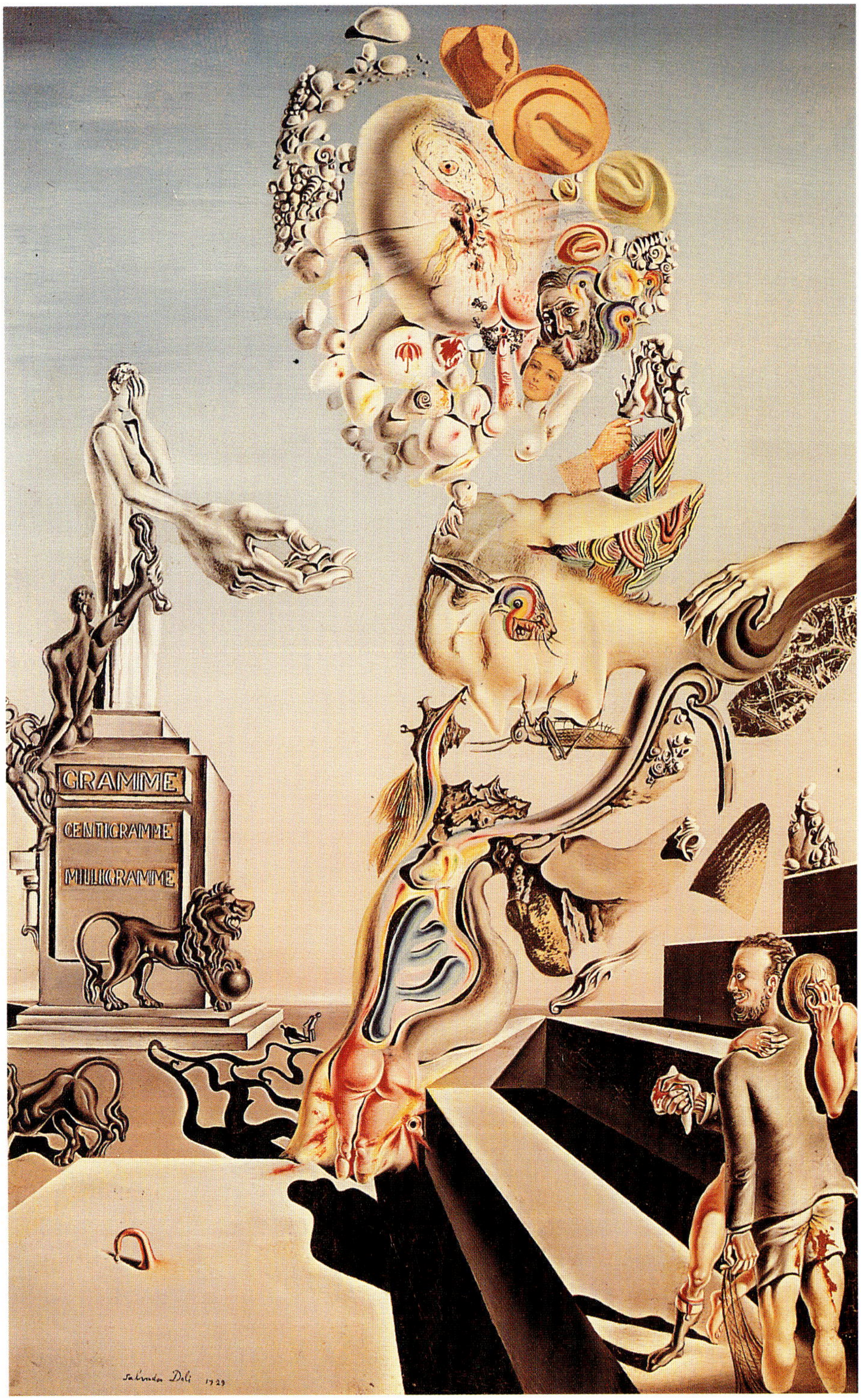

The Lugubrious Game ***(Le Jeu Lugubre)*****, 1929** (Private Collection). Often described as Dalí's most scatological work, this painting, only just over a foot wide, makes skilful use of a monochrome landscape to highlight the disturbing images of the dreaming mind. It is also known under the title *Dismal Sport*. Oil and collage on cardboard. 44.4 x 30.3 cm

In many of the paintings of this period scenes of masturbation feature prominently. *The First Days of Spring*, *The Lugubrious Game*, *Illumined Pleasures*, and *The Enigma of Desire*, all explore a dominant theme of sexual angst in a unique manner. Dalí had identified the grasshopper as a 'terrorizing element' of his childhood and it became crucial to the iconography of his paintings at this time, together with the image of the lion. By refusing to remain contented with the dream as a half-realized state subsequently shaped through a process of automatism, he had taken the Surrealist's ideal a step further and was well on his way to demonstrating his 'paranoiac-critical' theory. In *La Femme Visible*, a volume of his writings published in 1930, Dalí described this practice as 'a spontaneous method of irrational cognition based on the critical interpretative association of delusional phenomena'. He set out to infuse his dream images with a new visual ingredient, a 'paranoia', deliberately founded on a pattern of mental derangement which he attempted to systematize and control through the medium of his paintings. Instead of encouraging his dream images to surface through automatic drawing, Dalí began to procrastinate at the intersection of his real and imaginary worlds, producing fully formed images of waking dreams or hallucinations, with the intention of transcending a banal subjectivity in favour of a more expressive objective reality. He pursued his experiments at great cost to his own sanity.

Dawn Ades' critical study of the artist's work provides an excellent summary of Dalí's paintings of this exceptionally formative period. The pictures are made extraordinary, she writes, by the balance held between a 'real neurotic fear' and a 'knowing use of psychology textbooks'. She continues, '... the individual images that crowd into

The Great Masturbator, 1929 (Museo Nacional Centro de Arte Reina Sofía, Madrid). The central figure of the picture is that of Dalí himself, depicted as a soft, yellow, amorphous creature, out of which appears a cluster of sexual symbols – a woman's head positioned for fellatio and a male torso ready to receive her. It is Dalí's most anguished picture of this series, illustrating clearly his closeness to a complete mental breakdown. Oil on canvas. 110 x 150.5 cm

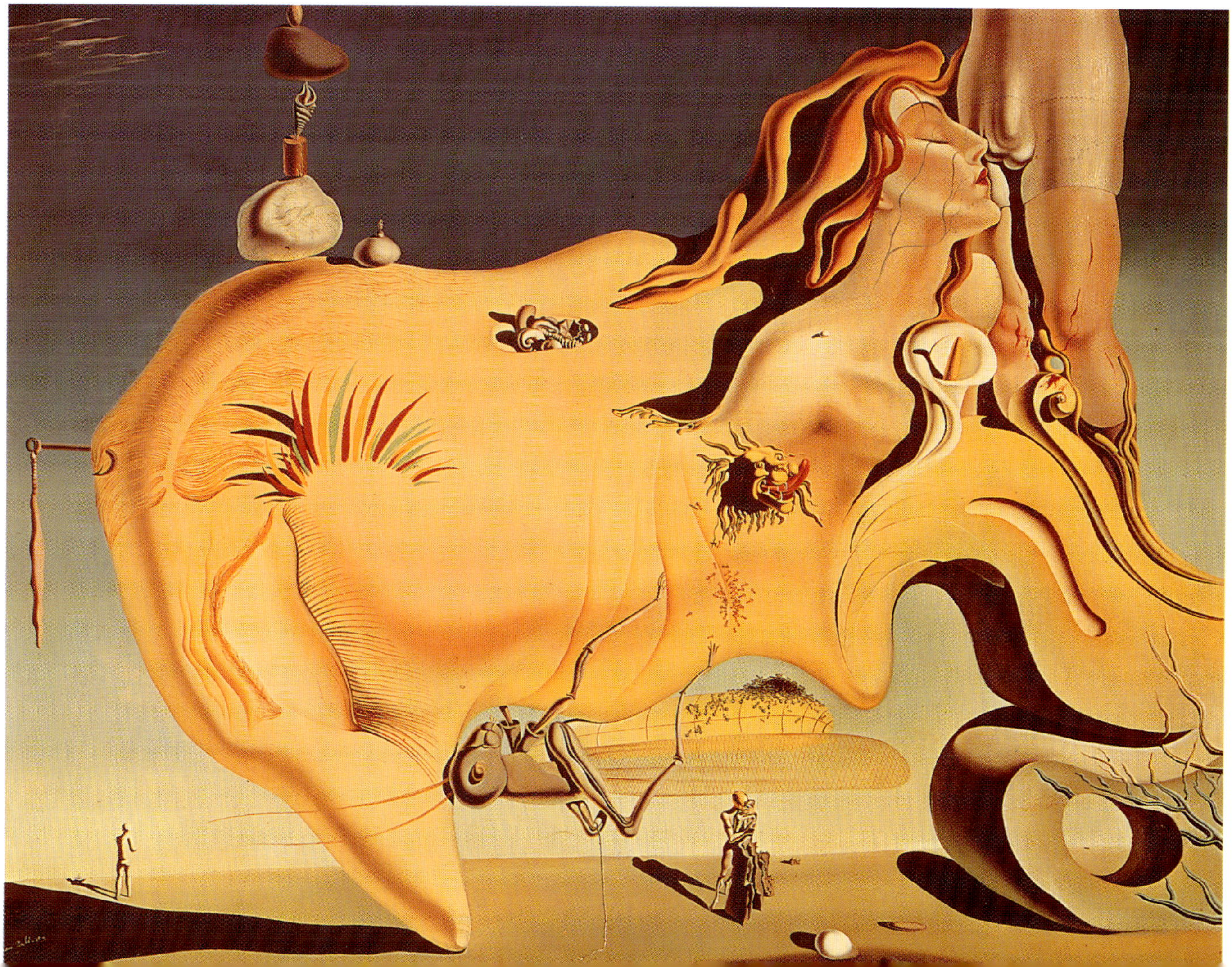

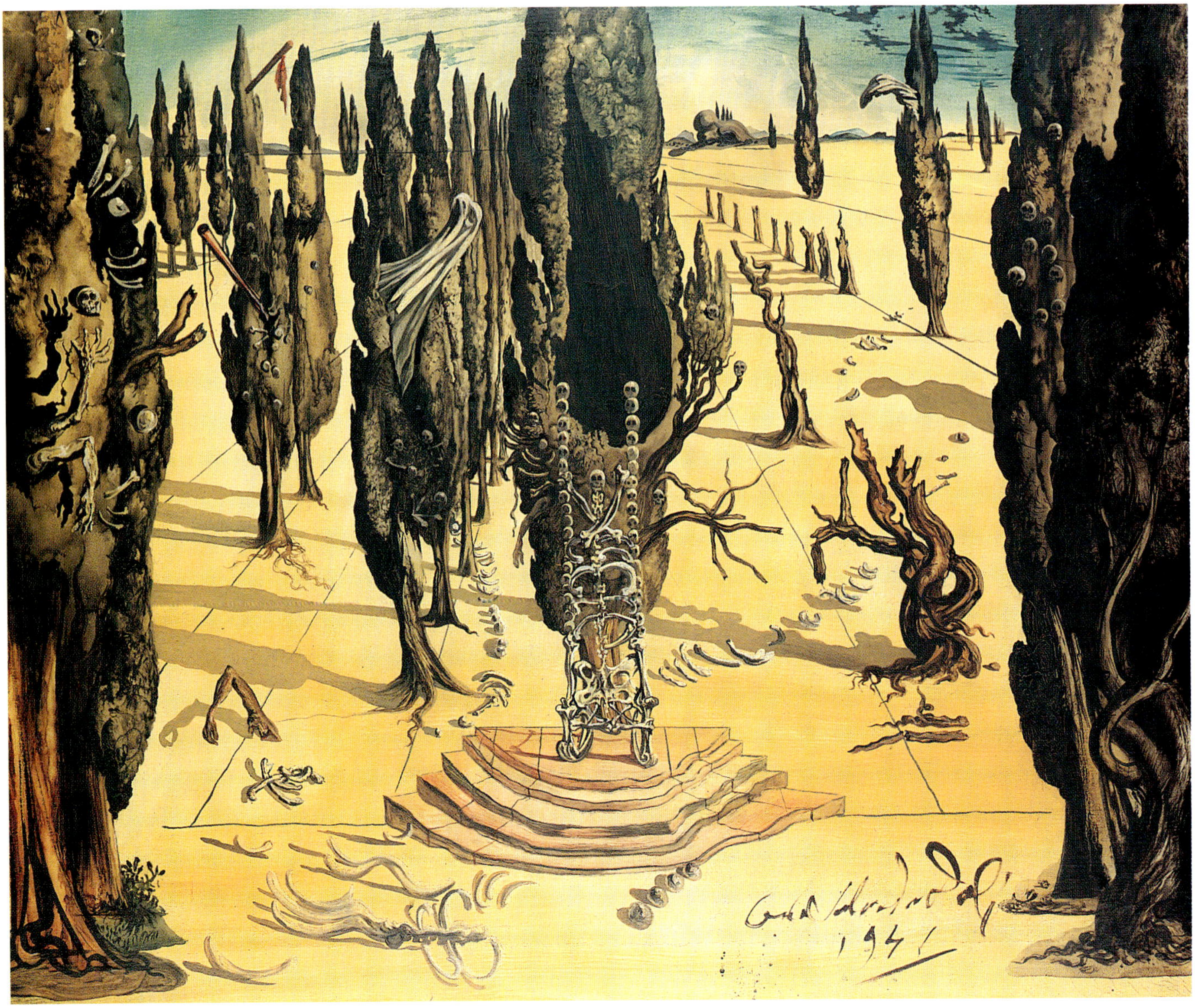

Tristan and Isolde ***(Tristan et Isolde)*****, 1941** (Private Collection). Dalí often adopted the practice of adding Gala's name to his Surrealist canvases. This painting, on a theme he was to return to for the ballet *Bacchanale*, bears the inscription Gala Salvador Dalí. Oil on canvas. 64 x 79 cm

the paintings are autobiographical, frequently symbolic, and often ready-interpreted. But the symbolic images he chooses are of different kinds: some are commonplaces from the psychology textbooks; some, like the grasshopper or fish, belong to Dalí's own personal armoury of images ... whose significance is made clear through juxtaposition and association in a series of paintings and through his own explanations; and others, like the deer, whose significance, if any, remains buried deep.'

Within a few weeks of arriving in Cadaqués, Dalí was visited by a group of Surrealist friends, including René and Georgette Magritte, Paul Eluard and his wife, Gala, Luis Buñuel, and Camille Goemans. These friends had known Dalí from his Parisian days as an 'unusual personality', but they were now shocked by his behaviour and by the series of new canvases. From hour to hour, his fits of laughter had become more violent and the anxiety he caused his friends appeared to him 'as comical as everything else', for he knew perfectly well that he was 'laughing at the images' bombarding his mind. All day long, he forced himself to become a 'medium' looking at his paintings so that day-dream visions would enter him. Often he placed his canvases by his bed, trying to dream about them, making certain that they were his first waking image. *The Lugubrious Game* was a subject of particular distress to the group visiting him. To the bottom right of the painting a figure appears with excrement-stained underclothing. Fears began to circulate among them that Dalí might be coprophagic, i.e. partial to the idea of eating human excrement. Paul Eluard's wife, Gala, was nominated to confront Dalí on this issue. He abruptly told her that he was not, and in doing so, offered some explanation of the imagery. 'I consciously loathe that type of aberration as much as you can possibly loathe it,' he reassured her. 'But I consider scatology as a terrorizing element, just as I do blood, or my phobia for grasshoppers.'

Gala was not impressed by Dalí to begin with. If anything, she felt that she and her husband had flattered the young Spaniard by their visit. She thought he possessed a 'professional Argentine tango slickness', with his mascaraed eyes and peculiar waxed moustache, and initially considered his outbursts of laughter exhibitionist and childish. Through Eluard, Gala had formed a long-standing relationship with the Surrealists and was referred to as the 'Surrealist Muse'. In his book *Revolutionaries without Revolution*, André Thirion, an influential member of the Surrealist movement, sketches the following portrait of the Gala Dalí met and rapidly fell in love with:

> *Gala knew what she wanted, the pleasures of the heart and the senses, money and the companionship of genius. She wasn't interested in politics or philosophy. She judged people by their efficiency in the real world and eliminated those who were mediocre, yet she could inspire the passions and exalt the creative forces of men as diverse as Ernst, Eluard and Dalí.*

Dalí began to take an exceptional interest in Gala. He saw in her the personification of the Russian girl with whom he had always felt himself in love. He had already painted Gala, he believed, in his earlier female portraits. 'Her body', he wrote in *The Secret Life*, 'was as delicate as that of a child ... the hollow of her back was extremely feminine and gracefully linked the energetic and proud torso to the very fine hips which the exaggerated slenderness of her waist made even more desirable.' Dalí began working on his portrait of Paul Eluard and Gala started to take him more seriously. When Eluard was obliged to return to Paris , Gala remained behind with Dalí and their relationship intensified dramatically. On one of their numerous long walks along the cliffs at Cape Creus, Dalí confessed to Gala, between fits of laughter, that he had fallen in love with her. 'But instead of being wounded by my laughter, Gala felt elated by it,' he recalls in *The Secret Life*. 'With her medium-like intuition she had understood the exact meaning of my laughter, so inexplicable to everyone else. She knew that my laughter was altogether different from the usual "gay" laughter. No, my laughter was not scepticism; it was fanaticism. My laughter was not frivolity; it was cataclysm, abyss, and terror. And of all the terrifying outbursts of laughter that she had already heard from me this, which I offered her in homage, was the most catastrophic, the one in which I threw myself to the ground at her feet, and from the greatest height! She said to me, "My little boy! We shall never leave each other."'

After meeting Gala, Dalí's hysterical symptoms 'disappeared one by one' and he began to prepare in earnest for his first Paris exhibition in November 1929 at the Camille Goemans Gallery. All of the disturbing pictures he had painted over the summer were exhibited, totalling eleven canvases, including his now finished portrait of Paul Eluard and perhaps his most demented work of the summer, *The Great Masturbator.* Dalí offers an interpretation of this particular painting in *La Femme Visible,* in poetic verse:

In spite of the general darkness
The evening had scarcely begun
At the edge of the great agate staircases
Where
Wearied by the light of day
Which had lasted since sunrise
The great masturbator
His immense nose resting on the onyx parquet
His enormous eyelids closed
His forehead riven by frightful wrinkles
And his neck swollen by the famous boil boiling with ants
Rested
Encounter in this still too bright evening hour
While the membrane which covers his mouth completely
Toughens under the agony of the enormous locust
Which had been gripped and glued to it
For five days and five nights

For the first time Dalí was publicly associated with the Surrealists. The exhibition was introduced by its leader André Breton who acknowledged in the paintings an originality and genius comparable only to the 1923-4 works of Max Ernst. This opinion was not unanimously upheld among the movement's members, however. Another leading Surrealist, Georges Bataille, saw 'an appalling ugliness' in *The*

The Bleeding Roses *(Les Roses Sanglantes)*, 1930 (Private Collection). Several of Dalí's canvases between 1927 and 1935 explore a theme of the artist's terror of the eternal feminine and, in particular, a fear of female sexuality. Here, his acute panic manifests itself in an image of a nude with bleeding roses sprouting from her womb. Oil on canvas. 60 x 48 cm

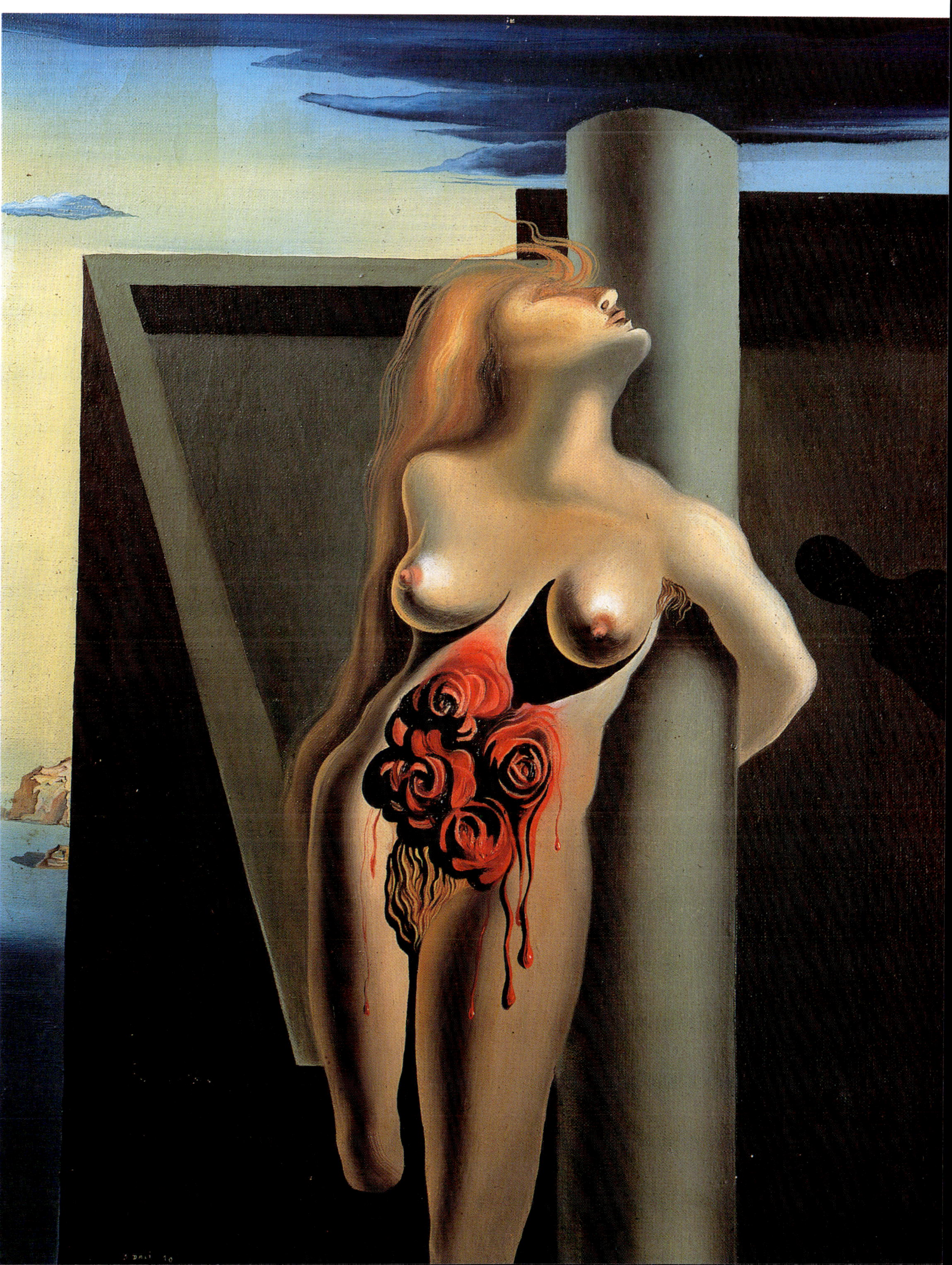

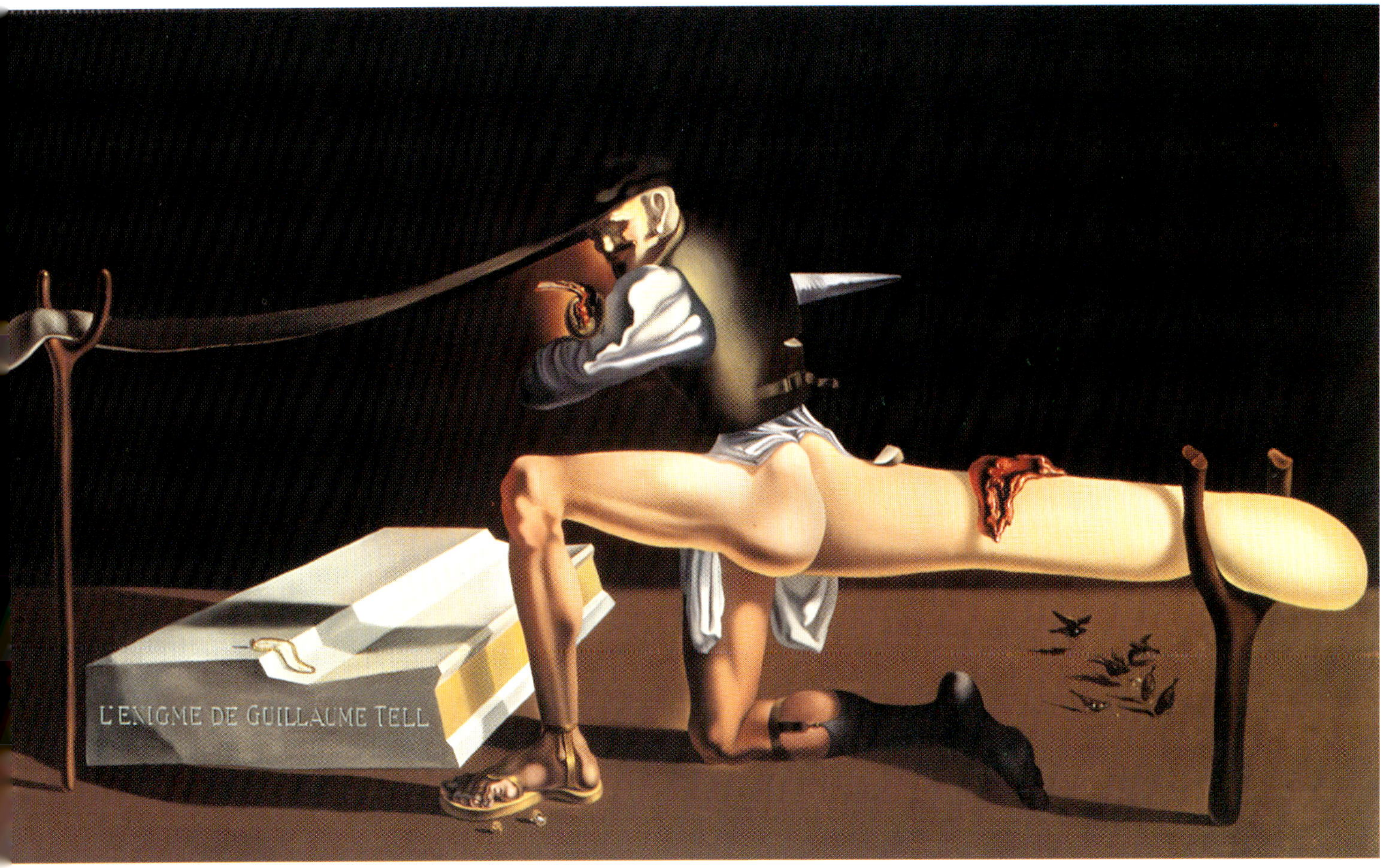

The Enigma of William Tell *(L'énigme de Guillaume Tell)*, 1933 (Museum of Modern Art, Stockholm). The threat from the father figure was the subject of a number of extremely large canvases from this period. The dark background adds to the sinister Lenin figure leering at his child, depicted as a cutlet of meat, whom he is about to devour. Oil on canvas. 201.5 x 346.5 cm

Lugubrious Game and criticized the 'shameful and repellent' behaviour of its figures. Dalí himself did not attend the showing of his work. The joint demonstration of his talents through his exhibition and the release of his film, *Un Chien Andalou,* the previous month, left him feeling utterly satisfied that he had now conquered Paris. Gala had decided to devote herself exclusively to the man she now recognized as a genius. She became both his inspiration and his source of control. Without Gala, Dalí's genius may well have been powerless to express itself through his art; her patience and determination defeated the madness which threatened to overrun him. The two travelled via Barcelona to Sitges for their 'honeymoon' before Dalí returned to Figueres to confront his father, who impatiently awaited an explanation of what he had judged his son's recently 'piggish behaviour'.

The Bitter Image of William Tell

A number of circumstances prompted Dalí's final separation from his father in January 1930, followed by the introduction of new, less autoerotic themes into his paintings. In the first instance, Don Salvador entirely disapproved of Dalí's liaison with a married woman ten years his senior whom he referred to as 'la madame' and with whom he associated the whole decadent influence of the Surrealists on his son. He had also read a review, printed in a Barcelona daily newspaper, of Dalí's Paris exhibition. Its author, the Spanish critic Eugeni d'Ors, stated that Dalí had inscribed his canvas *The Sacred Heart* with the words 'Sometimes I spit for pleasure on the portrait of my mother.' When challenged by his father, Dalí refused to retract the 'insult', arguing that 'in a dream one can commit a blasphemous act against someone whom one adores in real life ... In some religions, spitting is a sacred act.' Don Salvador, 'for reasons of dignity', immediately threw his son out of the house. Dalí reacted by shaving all his hair off. 'But I did more than this,' he wrote, 'I went and buried the pile of my black hair in a hole I had dug on the beach for this purpose ... Having done this I climbed up on a small hill from which one overlooks the whole village of Cadaqués and there, sitting under the olive trees, I spent two long hours contemplating that panorama of my childhood, my adolescence, and of my present.'

Forced to turn his back on Cadaqués, Dalí returned to Paris and to Gala, taking with him his two unfinished canvases, *The Invisible Man* and *Imperial Monument to the Child-Woman*. The collaboration with Buñuel on a second film, *L'Age d'Or, (The Golden Age)* did not go according to plan and Buñuel decided to complete the project on his own. When the film eventually opened in November 1930, it added hugely to Dalí's fame, although he felt that Buñuel had entirely betrayed him, having compromised all of his ideas, to produce a work whose originality was suffocated by a pathetic anticlericalism. Dalí now spent the majority of his time integrating with the Surrealists and socializing with the more prominent figures of high society. He was introduced to his first real patrons, the Viscount and Viscountess Charles and Marie-Laure de Noailles, who had already purchased *The Lugubrious Game*. He agreed to paint a new canvas for them and, with the money received in advance, he travelled back to Cadaqués in the hope of purchasing a home there for himself and Gala.

Dalí produced two outstanding paintings on the theme of his sundered relationship with his father, *The Old Age of William Tell,* the canvas commissioned and already paid for by the de Noailles, and *The Enigma of William Tell.* Sigmund Freud had written that 'The hero is the man who resists his father's authority and overcomes it,' and Dalí set out to achieve this ambition through his painting. He began *The Old Age of William Tell* in the summer of 1930 and completed it the following year while in Paris. Don Salvador appears in the picture as a bearded hermaphrodite and the Gala-Dalí couple appear three times in the painting. The central image is of a weeping pair turning their backs on the father figure whose lower body is shielded by a stretch of cloth. The hermaphrodite is enjoying some sort of surreptitious sexual activity behind this covering. The lion, Dalí's symbol of fear and anxiety, also makes a silhouette appearance in the painting. He has given his father the facial features of the Bolshevic leader, Lenin, in the later canvas *The Enigma of William Tell*, which he completed in 1933. Dalí himself has provided the following explanation of the painting's imagery:

> *William Tell is my father and the little child in his arms is myself; instead of an apple I have a raw cutlet on my head. He is planning to eat me. A tiny nut by his foot contains a tiny child, the image of my wife Gala. She is under constant threat from this foot. Because if the foot moves only very slightly, it can crush the nut.*

The Magnetism of Port Lligat

Gala and Dalí were no longer welcome in Cadaqués and their search for a home was made extremely difficult by the fact that Don Salvador had successfully soured his son's name throughout the entire village. Dalí refused to make a permanent home in Paris, however. The plain of Ampurdan and the tiny fishing village of Cadaqués haunted him. As a child he had roamed every path and knew every backstreet of the village. The surrounding landscape which Dalí described as 'the most concrete and most objective in the world' was used consistently as the backdrop to the curious universe of his paintings. He was adamant that his eyes would 'never cease to take nourishment' in such a place of 'solitude, grace, sterility, elegy'. He turned to an old friend for help – a half-delirious old woman in the neighbouring village of Port Lligat named Lidia whom he had known since childhood. Lidia offered the couple an old tumble-down shack in which her sons had once stored their fishing nets. The shack overlooked the sun-scorched cliffs and rocks rising steeply from the little enclosed bay with its pebbled shore,

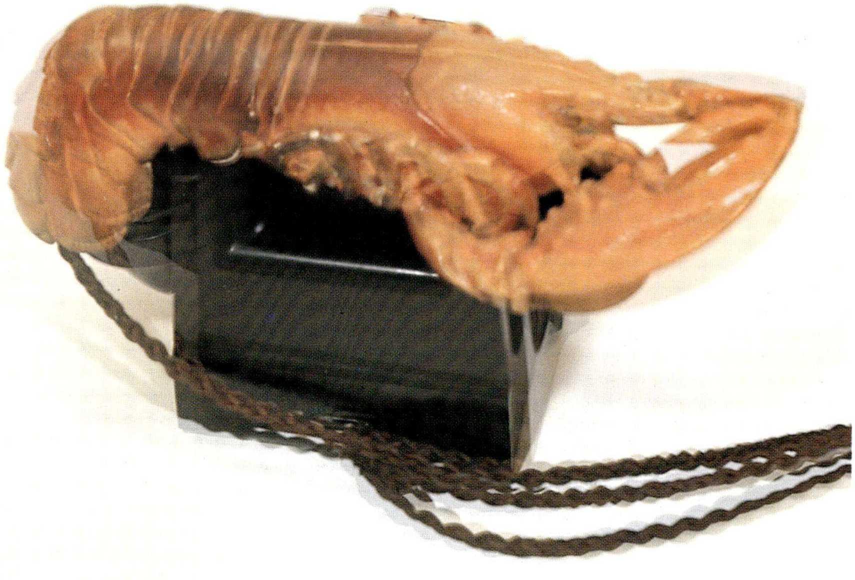

Lobster Telephone (Tate Gallery, London). Dalí was first struck by the notion that lobsters should replace telephones in 1935 and went on to develop this obsession in *The Secret Life,* demanding to know why, when he asked for a grilled lobster in a restaurant, he was never presented with a telephone. The model, displayed in a glass case in the Tate Gallery was made in Belgium by the Bell Company, while the handset was made in London.

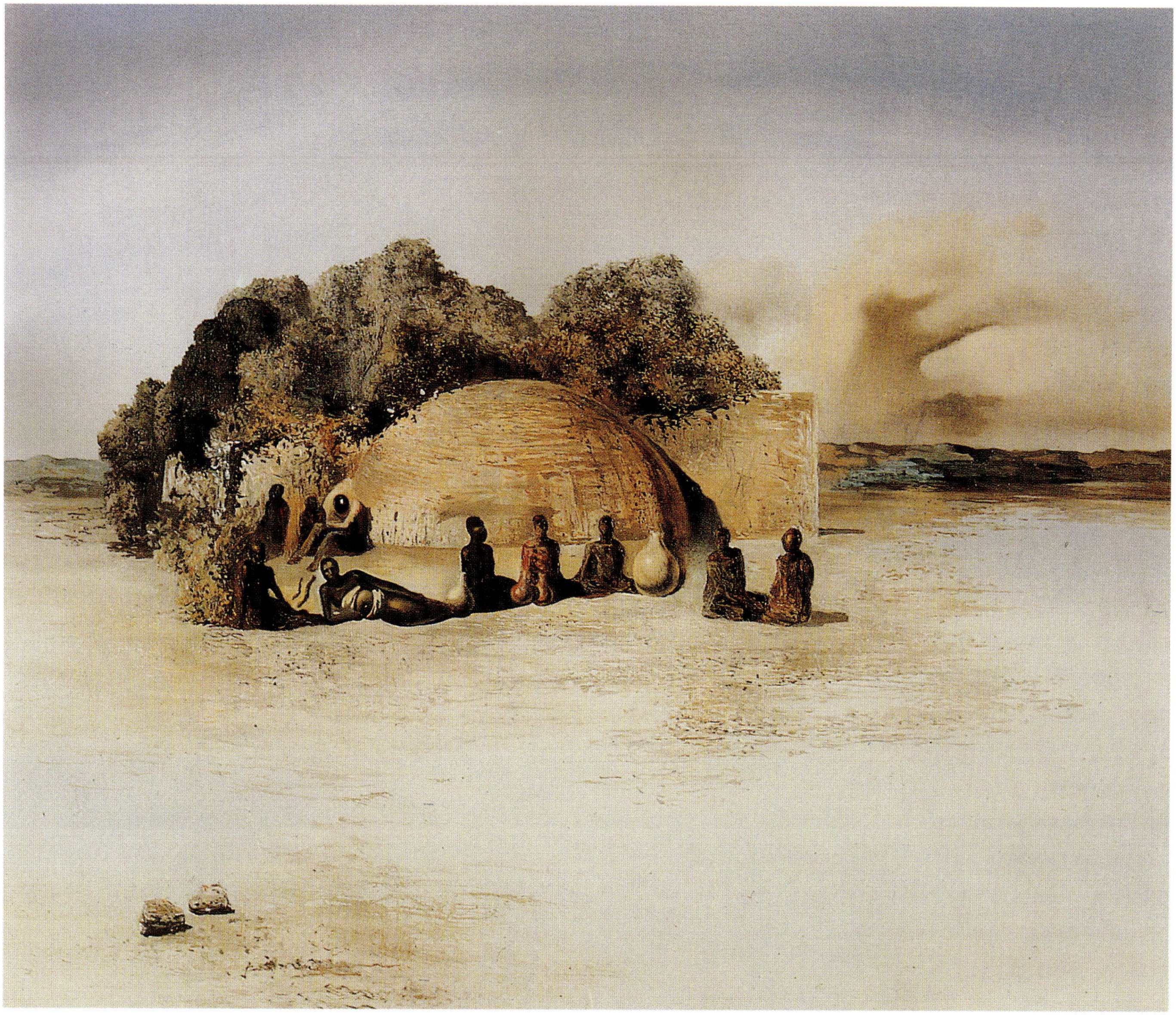

and the village itself was already home to a variety of eccentrics and social outcasts. The location appealed to Dalí's artistic sensibilities. He often referred to it as 'one of the most barren spots in the world' and it seemed to reflect the polarity of his personality. The mornings had a 'savage and harsh gaiety', the evenings were 'morbidly melancholy, grey, motionless'. Dalí and Gala made their permanent home in Port Lligat, adding rooms to the shack until it stretched across a considerable expanse of land.

Dalí was extremely active during the period 1930 to 1934. His time was divided between Port Lligat, where the couple stayed each year from the spring until early autumn, and Paris, where they returned each winter to re-establish close contact with the Surrealists. In the winter of 1930, Dalí helped to found the magazine *Le Surréalisme au Service de la Révolution* with André Breton. The magazine, which

Paranoiac Figure ***(Figure Paranoiaque)*****, 1934-5** (Private Collection). A first version of this painting appeared in *Le Surréalisme au Service de la Révolution* in December 1931 to coincide with the evolution of Dalí's paranoiac-critical theories. Oil on wood panel. 14.5 x 22.5 cm

was replaced by *Minotaure* in 1933, published countless articles written by Dalí, including two outstanding ones on Art Nouveau and the architecture of Antonio Gaudi. Dalí also participated in numerous Surrealist shows and lectures, while at the same time managing to publish *La Femme Visible, L'Amour et la Mémoire,* and *Conquest of the Irrational.* His first one-man Paris exhibition was held at the Pierre Colle gallery in June 1931. It was both a financial and critical success, and led directly to the artist's meeting with a man destined to make him famous in America. A young art dealer named Julien Levy had attended the Pierre Colle exhibition and had returned to America with *The Persistence of Memory,* a canvas he purchased for $250. He held a small exhibition of Dalí's work in New York in November of that same year. It sparked off an interest in him which grew rapidly, ultimately presenting him with the opportunity to earn vast amounts of money, an ambition Dalí was never shy to acknowledge publicly.

The paintings spanning this period, before the official break with the Surrealist movement, demonstrate the development and maturing of Dalí's systematization of obsessions through his paranoiac-critical method. The majority of them translate images of the places around Cadaqués and Port Lligat. Such works as *The Average Fine and Invisible Harp, The Spectre of Sex Appeal, The Weaning of Furniture Nutrition,* and *The Ghost of Vermeer of Delft, Which Can Be Used As a Table,* all contain faithful reproductions of the landscape. The painting *Persistence of Memory – Soft Watches,* completed in 1931, introduced a new element to Dalí's work – the development of his 'morphological aesthetics of soft and hard'. Two factors influenced this turn of events. He would often spend long hours meditating the rocks at Cape Creus which he considered a 'true geological delirium', capable of demonstrating the 'principle of paranoiac metamorphosis'. It was Dalí's belief that these rocks could often bear a haunting resemblance to things they were not. Gala also played a vital role, he asserts in *The Secret Life.* 'Instead of hardening me, as life had planned, Gala ... succeeded in building for me a shell to protect the tender nakedness of the Bernard the Hermit that I was, so that while in relation to the outside world I assumed more and more the appearance of a fortress, within myself I could continue to grow old in the soft, and in the supersoft. And the day I decided to paint watches, I painted them soft.' In the foreground of the picture, contrasting sharply with the jagged cliffs of the background, the same disturbing, soft figure who appears in *The Great Masturbator* lies with his nose pressed into the ground. The melancholic twilight landscape of Port Lligat features as the backdrop for the surprising image of the limpid watches, which Dalí, in his own words, described as 'no more than paranoiac-critical camemberts – extravagant, solitary, the camemberts of time and space'.

Atmospheric Chair, 1934 (Chicago Art Institute). During the early 1930s, Dalí developed a particular fixation for chairs, depicting them as 'irrational objects' on canvas, or designing them as 'Surrealist objects with symbolic functions' so that nobody could sit on them. Oil on wood. 18 x 14 cm

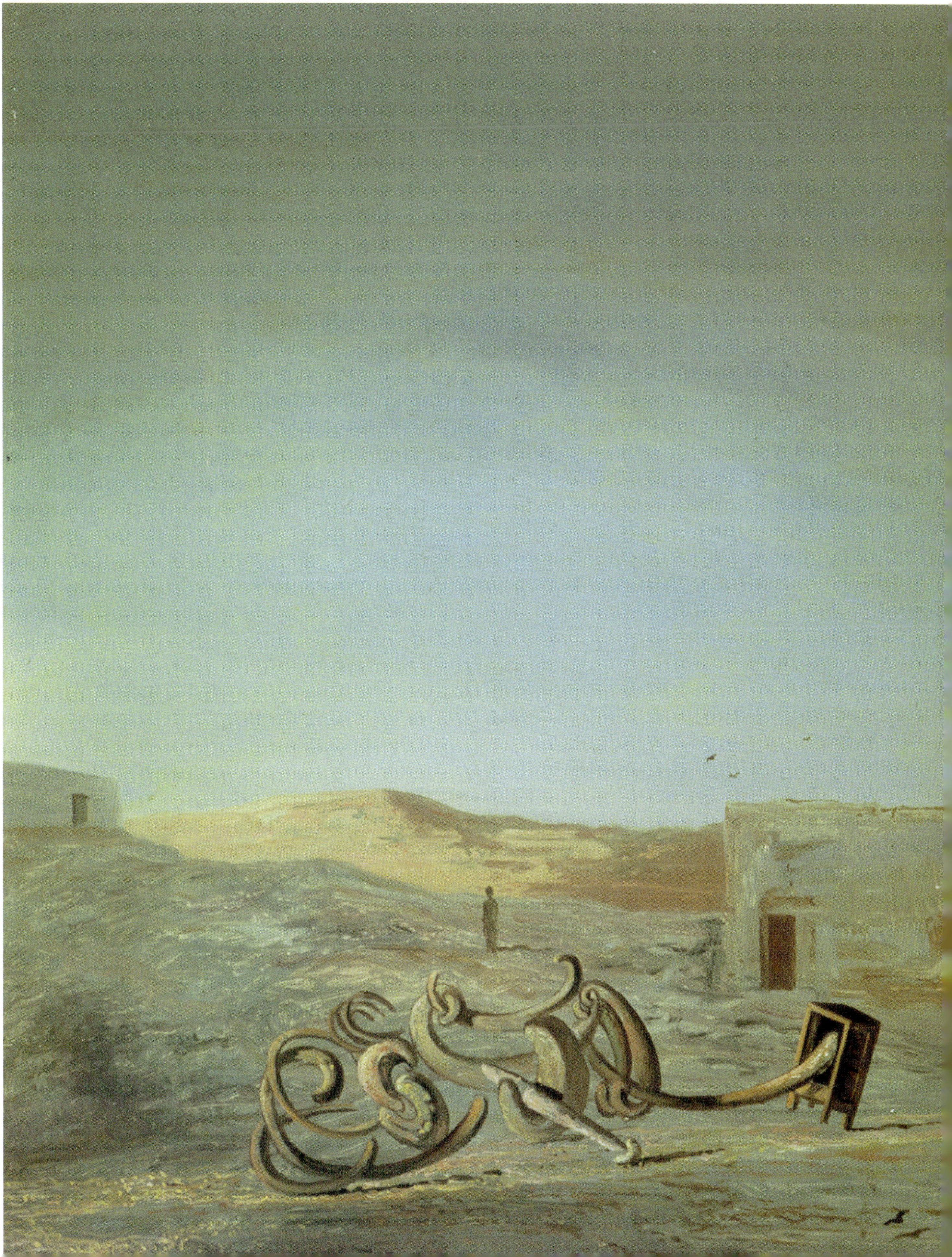

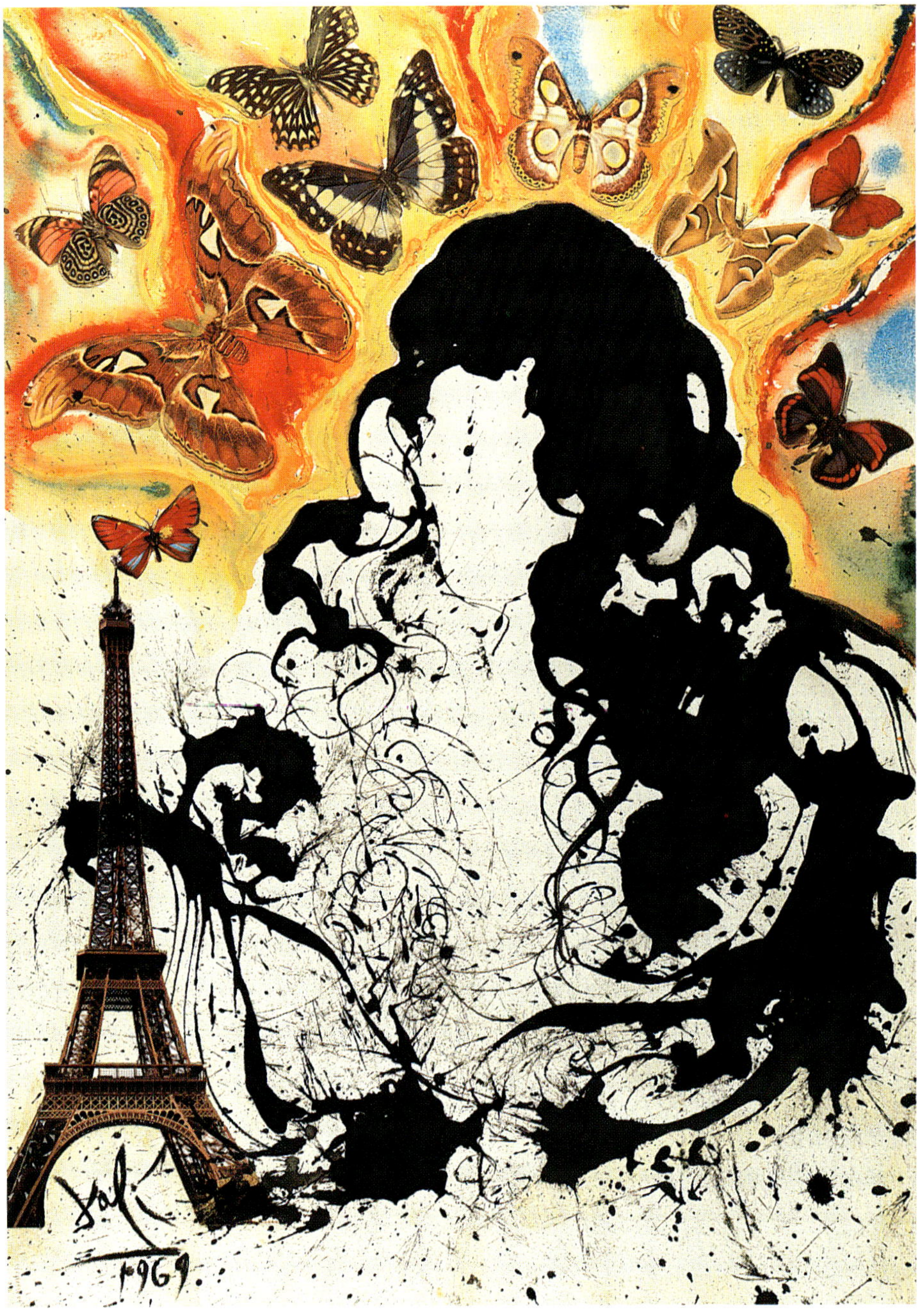

Eiffel Tower and Louis XIV (Private Collection). Completed in 1969, this later canvas has a distinctly French theme and combines three separate media. The outline of Louis XIV's head is in ink. The background colour is in watercolour on top of which is added the collage of the Eiffel Tower.
77.5 x 56.5 cm

Dalí's Surrealist Artefacts

While he still continued to paint his Surrealist canvases, Dalí began to cultivate the practice of endowing certain objects with symbolic Surrealist significance, with the intention of further eroding traditional concepts of logic. He enlisted the help of the sculptor, Alberto Giacometti, for this purpose, insisting that 'the surrealist object had created a new need of reality. People no longer wanted to hear the "potential marvellous" talked about. They wanted to touch the "marvellous" with their hands'. Dalí believed that the fashion he had now created had 'killed elementary Surrealist painting'. In *The Secret Life*, Dalí describes two of the delirious and obsessive objects he set about creating. The first was a loaf of bread, transformed into a form of crypt.

> *One day I hollowed out entirely an end of a loaf of bread, and what do you think I put inside it? I put a bronze Buddha, whose metallic surface I completely covered with dead fleas ... After putting the Buddha inside the bread I closed the opening with a little piece of wood, and I cemented the whole, including the bread, sealing it hermetically in such a way as to form a homogeneous whole which looked like a little urn, on which I wrote 'Horse Jam'. What does that mean, eh?*

A second experiment involved the transformation of a chair into an object which provoked a 'profound uneasiness in all who saw it'. Dalí substituted the leather seat for one made of chocolate. He screwed a door knob under one of the chair legs and planted the other in a glass of beer. He christened this creation 'Atmospheric Chair'.

The Breach with the Surrealists

The Surrealists had begun to seriously reconsider Dalí's membership of the movement. The onslaught of turbulent ideas they had witnessed from him was now judged an affront to the movement. He had begun to exalt the paintings of the battle painter, Meissonier, an artist who had supported the most savage colonialism of his time. It seemed that Dalí would go to any extreme to provoke controversy, that he was intent on following a path of aesthetic terrorism. Fame had carried him to the point where he wrote, 'I was no longer master of my own legend, and henceforth Surrealism was to be more and more identified with me, and with me only ... The group I had known was in a state of complete disintegration. And a whole Surrealist faction, obeying the slogans of Louis Aragon, a nervous little Robespierre, was rapidly evolving toward a complete acceptance of the communist cultural platform.'

Aragon, who stood at the ethical core of the movement, could see nothing even vaguely amusing in Dalí's whimsical behaviour and he was appalled by the excess of scatology in the artist's paintings. Breton, for his part, had founded the movement only to have Dalí declare himself the only 'integral Surrealist'. Dalí had started to argue that he had been a Surrealist 'from birth', he rejected 'neither the blood nor the excrement that was in their manifestos'. In his *Diary of a Genius* he explained his expulsion by the fact that he had taken Surrealism too literally, 'so much so, that in the end I was expelled from the group because I was overly-Surrealistic'.

Dalí's Hitler mania was the final straw. The Surrealists had tolerated his Lenin, given a three-metre-long anamorphic buttock supported by a crutch, but they could not countenance his latest political subject. He had begun to have repeated dreams of Hitler dressed as a woman. He elaborated on these dreams many years later in conversations with André Parinaud:

> *His flesh, which I had imagined whiter than white, ravished me. I painted a Hitlerian wet nurse knitting sitting in a puddle of water ... There was no reason for me to stop telling one and all that to me Hitler embodied the perfect image of the great masochist who would unleash a world war solely for the pleasure of losing and burying himself beneath the rubble of an empire.*

Dalí believed that his Hitler fixation should have 'warranted the admiration of the Surrealists', given the fact that he was out to ridicule the gratuitous nature of Hitler's actions. Breton however, refused to believe that Dalí's obsession was some sort of demonstration of his peculiar brand of humour. The situation was not helped by the fact that, when required to defend the accusations hurled at him before the group in January 1934, Dalí appeared with a thermometer in his mouth, wearing several layers of clothing. He read out his address as he performed a striptease, peeling off his clothing article by article, while attempting to convince his friends that his attraction to Hitler was strictly paranoiac. He had always proclaimed that 'politics are merely historical anecdotes', but believed he did not have the right to exercise any control over the content of paintings inspired by his dreams. 'If Hitler were ever to conquer Europe,' he insisted 'he would do away with hysterics of my kind ... the effeminate and manifestly crackpot part I had cast Hitler in would suffice for the Nazis to damn me as an iconoclast.'

Dalí had the support of old friends, including Paul Eluard and Tristan Tzara, both of whom recognized that he would certainly need to find another subject for his delirium, but who argued with Breton that Dalí's involvement was absolutely crucial to the continuing success of the Surrealists. Breton was already confident, however, of a majority against Dalí's ongoing membership. He dismissed him with the statement:

> *Since Dalí had repeatedly been guilty of counter-revolutionary activity involving the celebration of fascism under Hitler, the undersigned propose ... that he be considered a fascist element and excluded from the Surrealist movement and opposed with all possible means.*

The Surrealists could not fail to acknowledge Dalí's remarkable contribution to their growth and development. Even if a great deal of

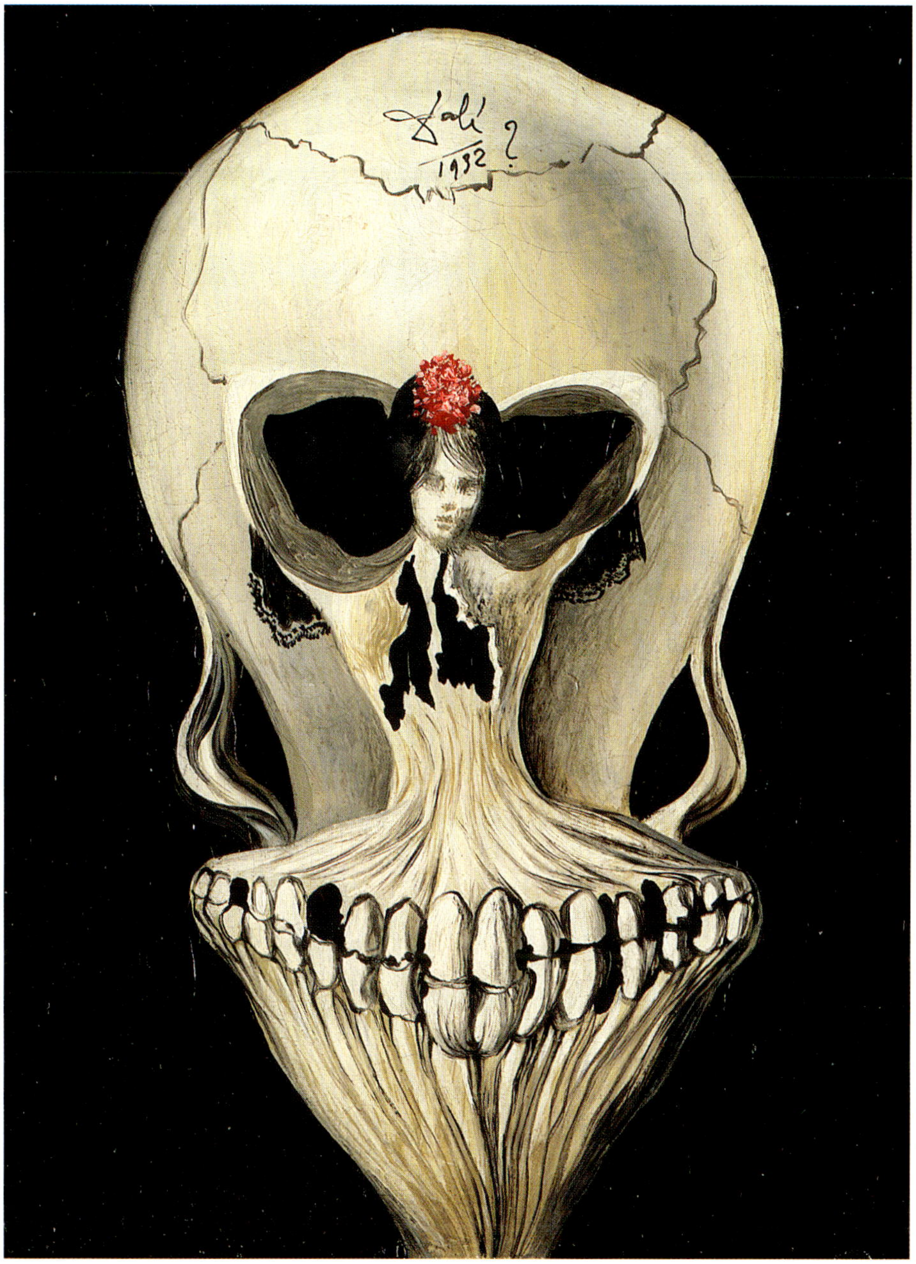

The Ballet Dancer ***(Ballerine)*** (Private Collection). Dalí's Surrealist interpretation of a ballerina painted in 1932, whose tutu merges with the jawbone of a skull. The sinister atmosphere is enhanced by the black and white contrast of colours. Oil on canvas. 57 x 70 cm

truth rested in Breton's statement that Dalí was an artist 'indifferent to the means by which he set out to make an impression', praise for his achievements was never in short supply. The dogmatic hard-liner, André Thirion, could himself offer the following objective assessment:

> *Dalí's contribution to Surrealism was of immense importance to the life of the group and the evolution of its ideology. Those who have maintained anything to the contrary have either not been telling the truth or have understood nothing at all. ... In spite of everything, what we are constantly seeing in his work is exemplary draughtsmanship, a startlingly inventive talent, and a sense of humour and of theatre. Surrealism owes a great deal to his pictures.*

CHAPTER 4

The Later Works

I have the universal curiosity of Renaissance men, and my mental jaws are constantly at work.

Les Passions selon Dalí

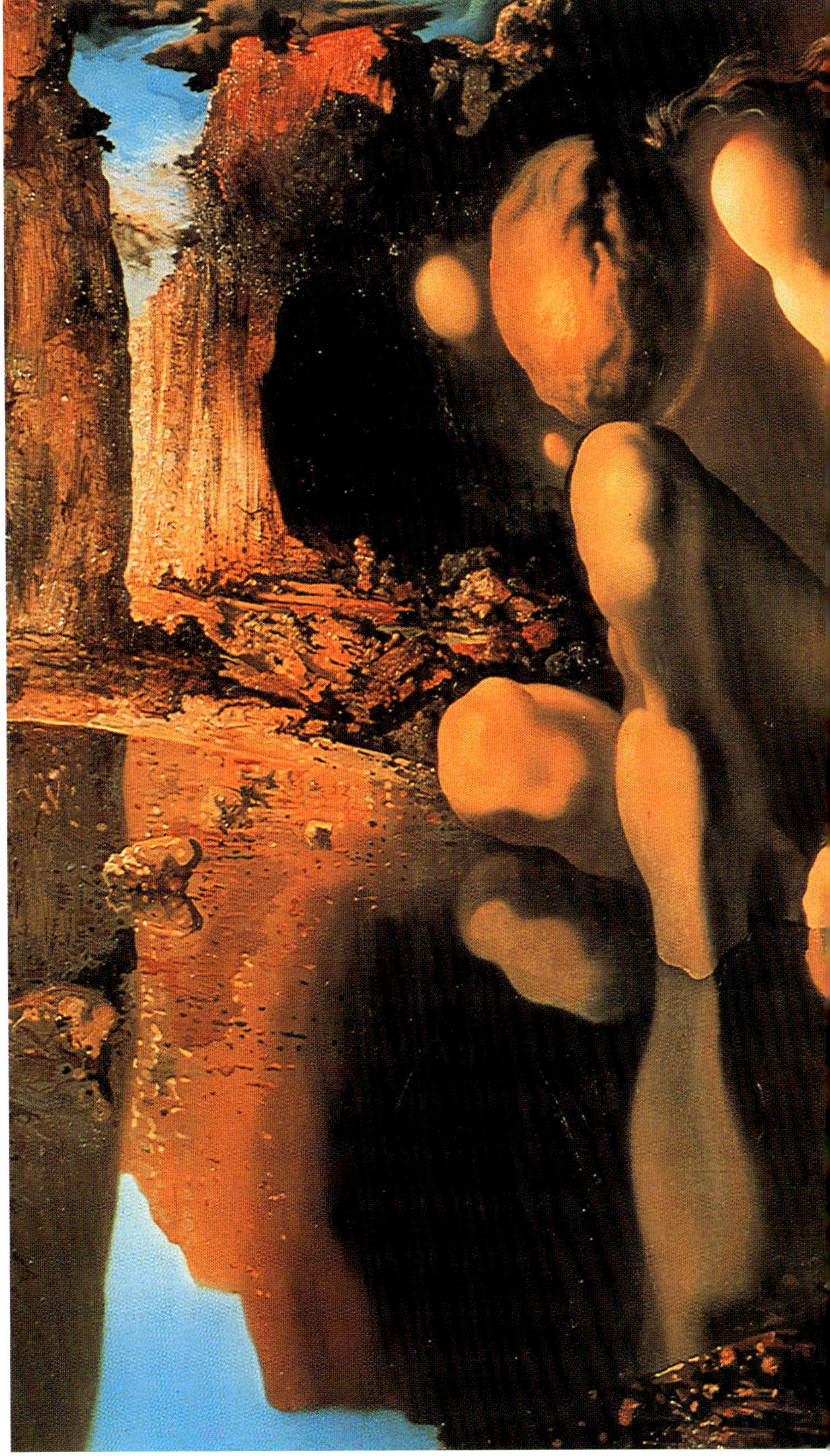

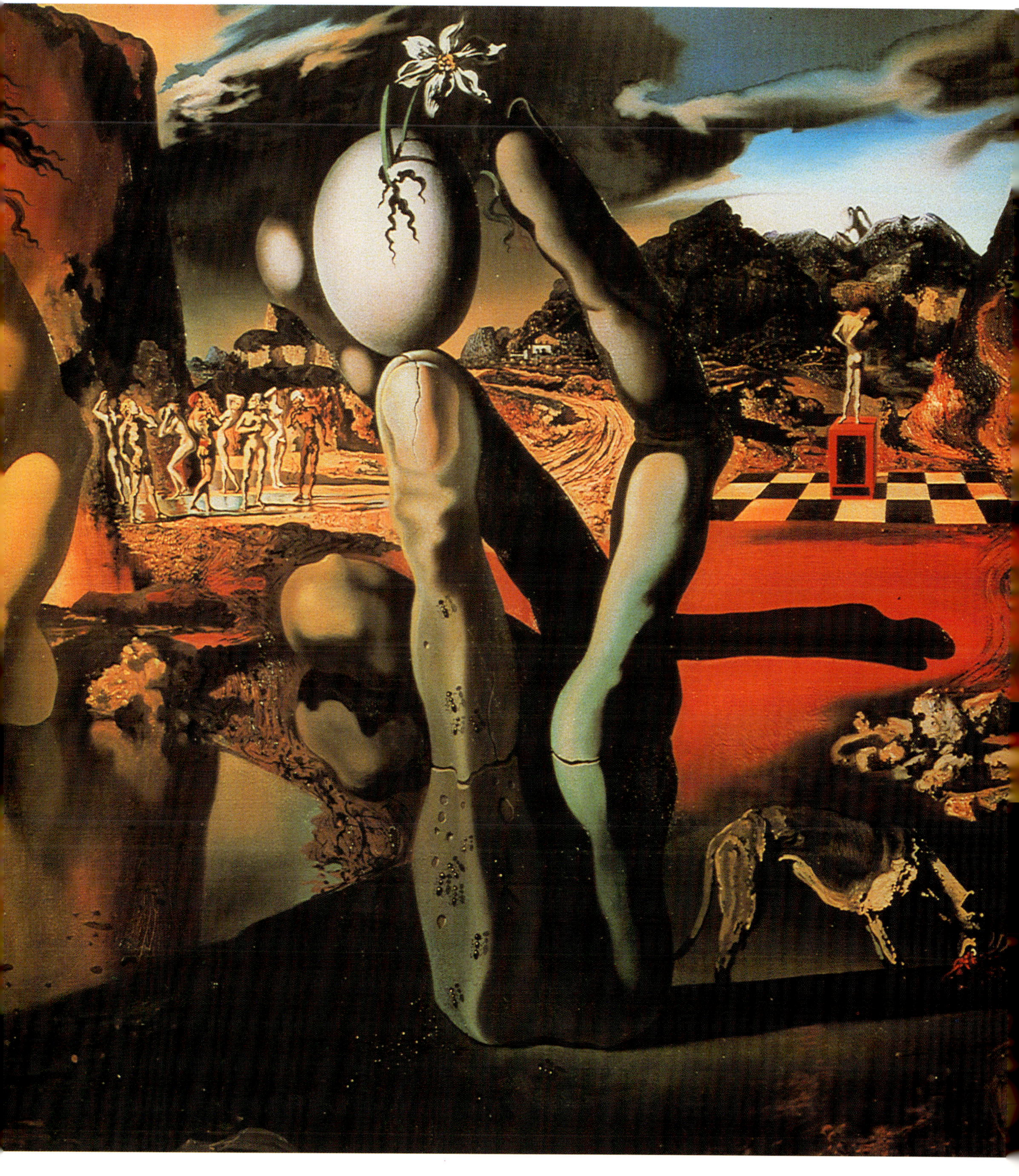

Overleaf:
Metamorphosis of Narcissus, 1937 (Tate Gallery, London). Dalí explained the imagery of this painting as the transformation of Narcissus into the image of a hand which suddenly rises from its own reflection. This hand holds an egg in its fingertips, a seed, the bulb from which the new Narcissus – the flower – is born. A long poem accompanied the painting. Oil on canvas. 50 x 76 cm

Dalí's decision to strike out independently of the Surrealists occurred at a time when he was simultaneously at the height of his reputation, yet at the low point of his financial resources. His predicament in this respect encouraged a period, leading up to the Second World War, when he was more determined than ever to build on his popularity and fame. America presented itself as a lucrative proposition, and the encouragement of friends such as Julien Levy and the American heiress, Caresse Crosby, cemented an image in Dalí's mind of a New World simply longing to accommodate his financial advancement.

Midas in America

Picasso had generously offered Dalí the money he and Gala needed to cross the Atlantic and the couple made their first trip to New York in November 1934. Upon arrival, a second exhibition of the artist's work was held at the Julien Levy Gallery. It was highly successful and many of Dalí's canvases sold to interested collectors at remarkably high prices. The American art world, and especially the Press, adored Dalí's eccentric personality and courted it at every opportunity. Caresse Crosby, who had accompanied the couple from Europe, saw to it that Dalí was introduced to the most influential socialites in New York. After this trip, lasting three months, he returned to Europe, richer by $5,000. He had formed the resolve to return frequently to the United States whenever his finances demanded it. Once he had re-installed himself in Port Lligat, he painted the famous canvas *Mae West's Face*, inspired by this first American visit, a portrait which the actress reputedly found 'highly amusing'.

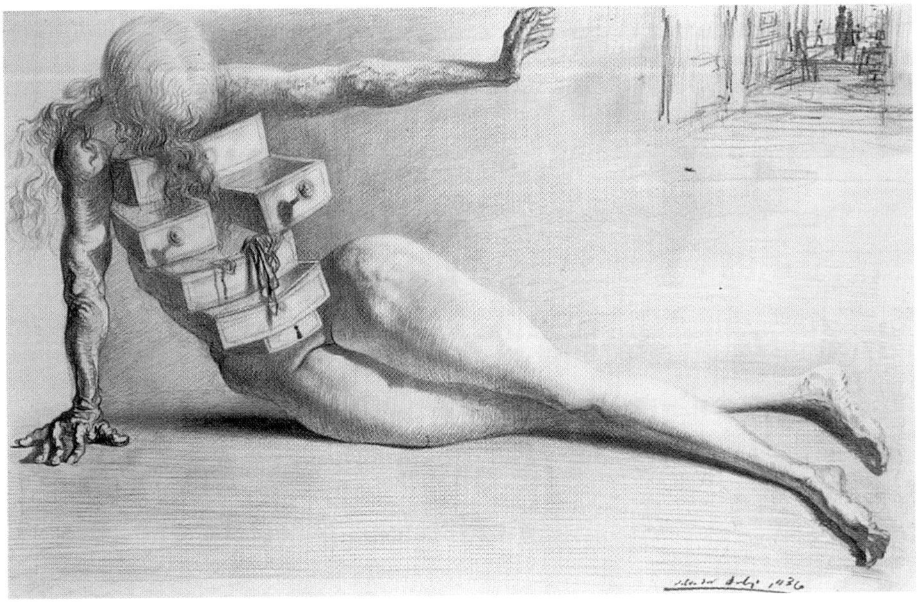

Right:
City of Drawers, 1936 (Chicago Art Institute). The idea behind this drawing, Dalí wrote, was to 'draw a kind of allegory of psychoanalysis representing a certain complacency in savouring the narcissistic odour of every one of our drawers'. Pencil on paper. Dimensions unknown.

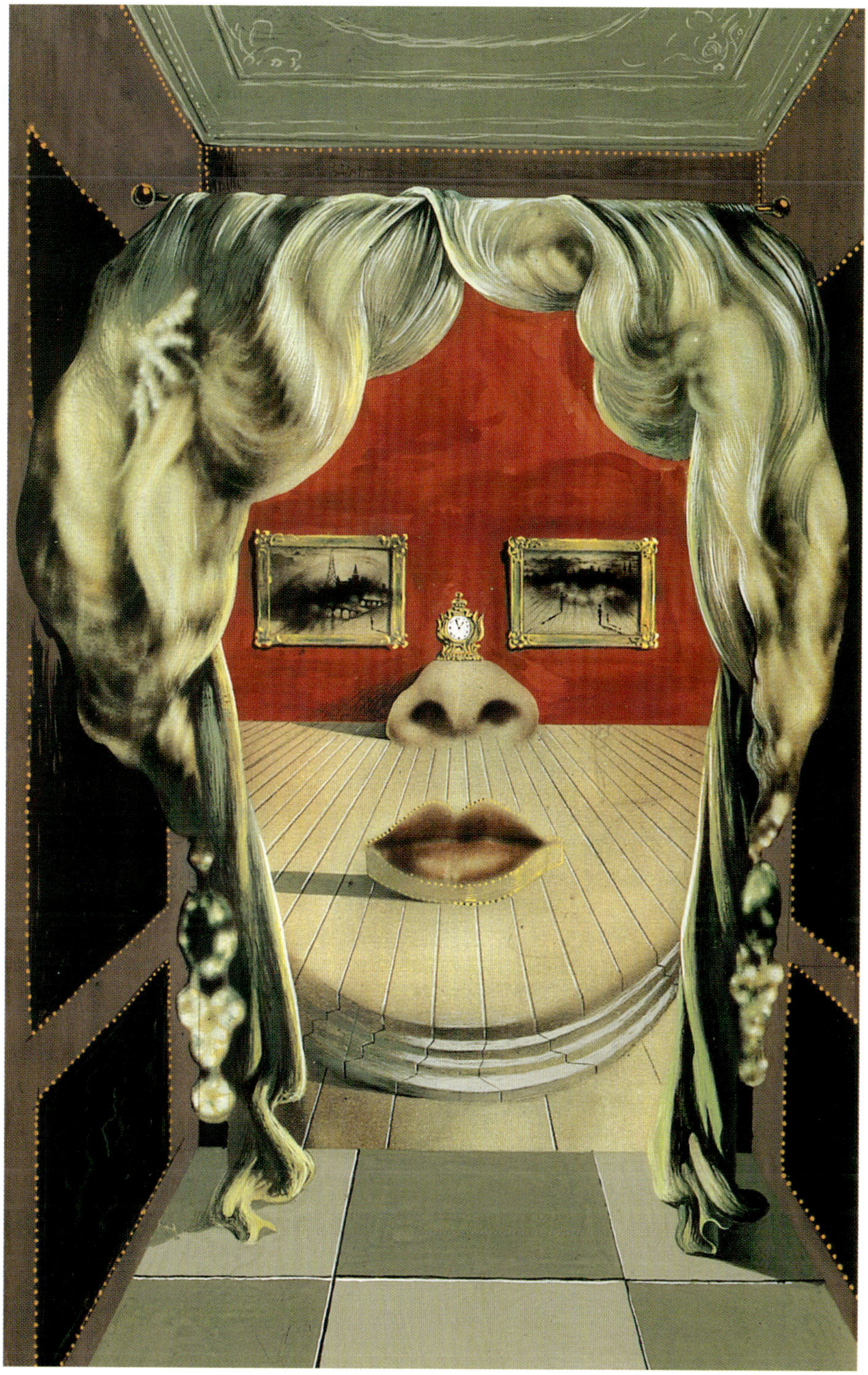

Mae West's Face Which Can be Used as a Surrealist Apartment, 1934-5 (Chicago Art Institute). On seeing this portrait, Mae West was reputedly keen to have her bathroom decorated in accordance with Dalí's image. The picture was produced in gouache on newspaper. 31 x 17 cm

Dalí also became well known in Britain at this time. He had met Edward James in 1933 at the home of the Viscount de Noailles. James, a godson of King Edward VII, was extremely rich and eventually acted as Dalí's English patron. The International Exhibition of Surrealism was held in London in June 1936. Dalí exhibited his paintings alongside the works of artists such as Miró, Magritte, Duchamp, di Chirico and Man Ray. It was at this event that he engineered perhaps

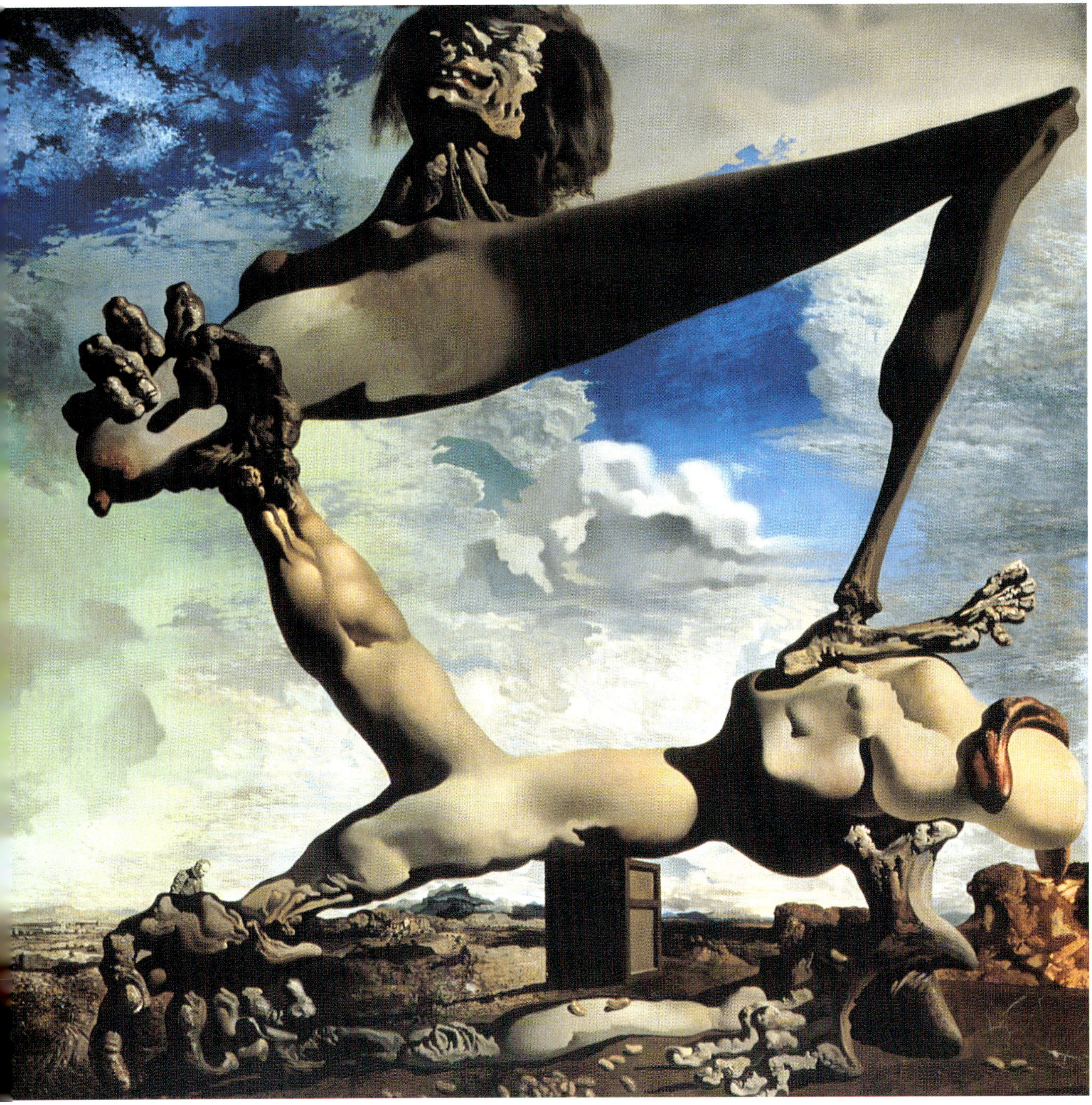

his greatest ever publicity stunt, albeit unintentionally. Dalí arrived at the Exhibition dressed in a diving suit and helmet but soon began to experience difficulty breathing inside the helmet. Spectators assumed that his writhing figure on stage was simply part of the eccentric performance they had come to expect from Dalí. He was rescued by James, having come close to death by suffocation.

Exile from Spain

Soft Construction with Boiled Beans: Premonition of Civil War, 1936
(Philadelphia Museum). Dalí painted this picture six months before the outbreak of the Civil War which is symbolized as one giant figure, with head and body struggling to rip away from each other. Dalí judged Spain to be both the victim and the aggressor. Violent internal rupturing is the theme of the painting. Oil on canvas. 110 x 84 cm

The outbreak of the Spanish Civil War in July 1936 forced Dalí to abandon his home at Port Lligat and for the next three years he lived in various countries throughout Europe. Six months before General Franco declared himself Spain's Head of State, Dalí had painted *Soft Construction with Boiled Beans – Premonition of Civil War.* The imagery of the painting, 'a huge human body, all arms and legs deliriously squeezing each other', is evidently turbulent, but the painting stands in marked contrast to the explicit horror of Picasso's *Guernica*. Dalí had always maintained that he was apolitical at heart and, unlike Picasso, he seems to have remained emotionally distant from the plight of those living through the Civil War. His old friend, Garcia Lorca, was arrested and shot by anti-Republican troops, but Dalí did not seem particularly moved by this event. He had once told the Surrealists that 'art should be edible' and he interpreted the war as a form of culinary fiasco, associated with the putrid smells of 'burned curates' fat and of quartered spiritual flesh, which mingled with the smell of hair dripping with the sweat of promiscuity ... of the mobs fornicating among themselves and with death'.

While in exile in Europe, Dalí became passionately involved in a diverse range of Surrealist enterprises and experiments. He made the acquaintance of several people in the higher echelons of the Paris fashion industry, including the avant-garde designers Coco Chanel and Elsa Schiaperelli. These individuals were the first to establish successful communication between the art and fashion worlds. Dalí began to design fabrics and a variety of bizarre hats in the shape of footwear, meat cutlets and inkwells. He also collaborated regularly with fashion magazines such as *Vogue, Harper's Bazaar* and *Town and Country*. In 1938, he travelled to London where he met Sigmund Freud and painted several portraits of him. He was delighted with Freud's remark that he had never before encountered 'a more complete example of a Spaniard. What a fanatic.'

Dalí lived in Italy for a considerable length of time during the political upheaval in Spain. The Italian artists he now encountered at first hand had an especially profound effect on his style of painting, for their influence first prompted a return to classicism, combined with mysticism, witnessed in the majority of his works from the early forties onwards. Dalí energetically visited the museums of Florence and Rome in the belief that 'a mediaeval period of reactualization of individual, spiritual and religious values' would eventually arise as a result of the collapse in Europe of both communism and fascism. He earnestly desired to become the architect of a new 'renaissance', with a 'full understanding of the laws of life and death of aesthetics'. *The Inventions of Monsters*, completed in 1937, was among several paintings of this period demonstrating the influence of the Italian Renaissance masters. Dalí explained that the foreground couple with the skull-like features holding the hourglass and the butterfly are a Pre-Raphaelite adaptation of the Gala-Dalí couple standing next to them. *The Metamorphosis of Narcissus* again uses a similar double image and draws on the symbolic imagery of early Renaissance art. The small gathering of dancing figures, for example, is clearly reminiscent of Sandro Botticelli, and the style of Dalí's painting imitates also Botticelli's great gift of lyrical precision.

The house at Port Lligat remained abandoned until 1948 when the couple returned from America after the Second World War. Dalí had left Europe for New York in 1939 and was present at the opening of another major exhibition of his work in March. Twenty-one of his paintings were sold at the event, earning him the vast sum of $25,000. In June of the same year he returned to France, but not before publishing his anti-art-establishment manifesto, entitled *Declaration of the*

Design for Vulcain and Venus *(Dessin pour Vulcain et Venus)*, 1941 (Private Collection). The three major ballets Dalí worked on during his exile in America included *Bacchanale, The Sentimental Colloquy* and *The Madness of Tristam*. He also made sketches for costumes, sets and collaborated on a number of librettos, not all of which reached public performance. Watercolour and gouache. 28 x 38 cm

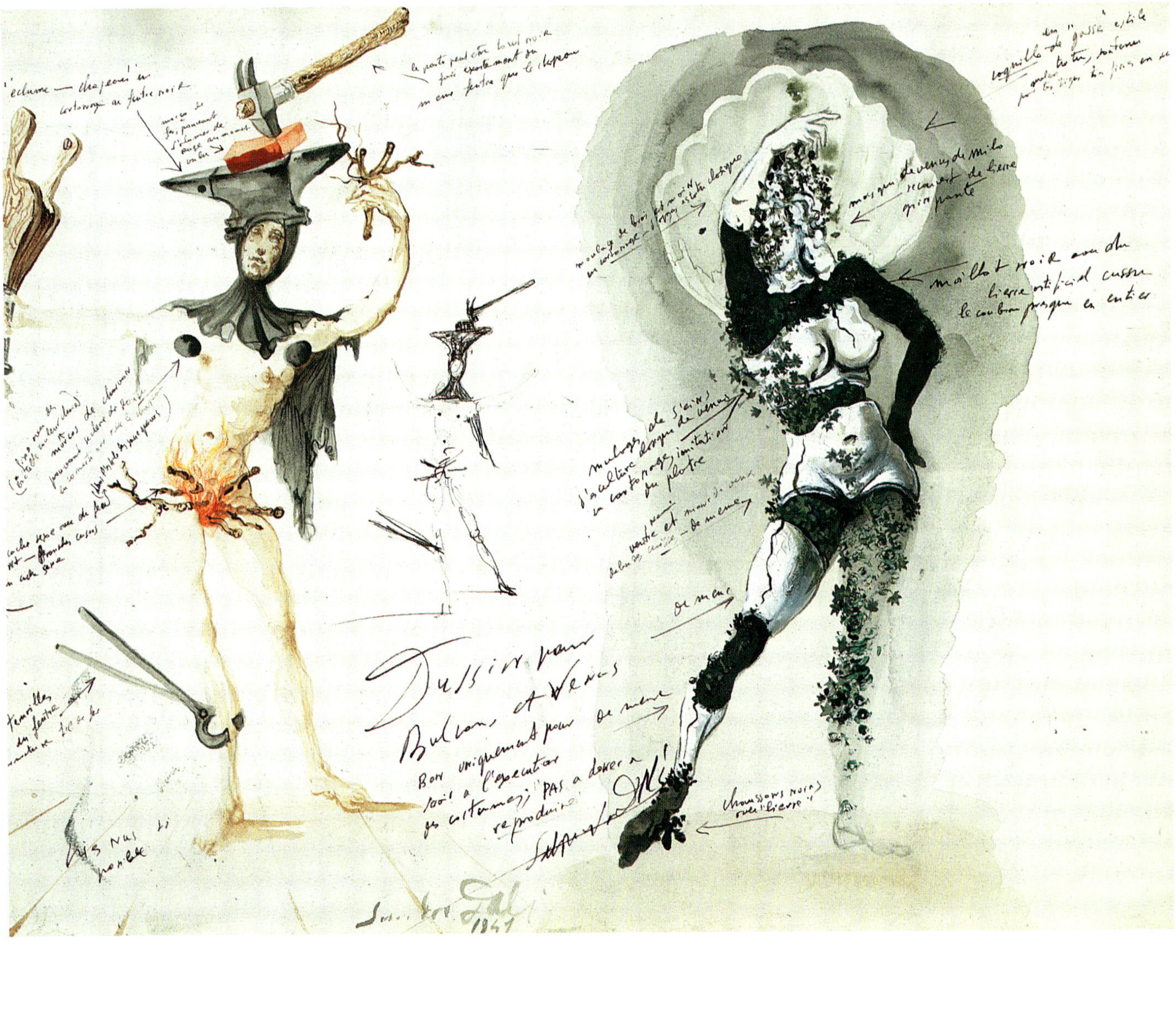

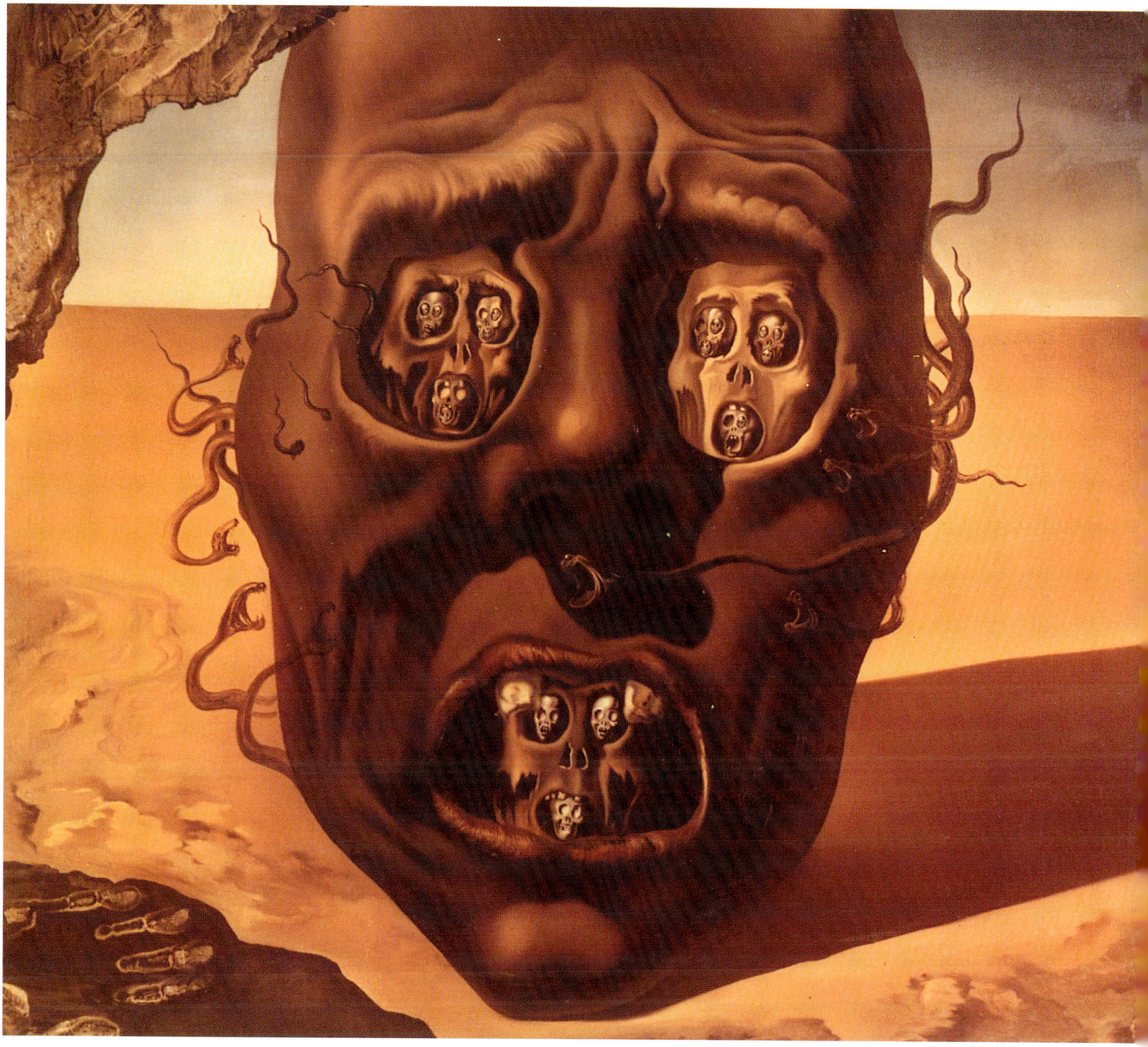

Independence of the Imagination and the Rights of Man to His Own Madness. The manifesto was prompted by his anger towards the Committee organizing the summer World Fair at Long Island where Dalí had designed a pavilion he named *Dream of Venus*. The entrance to the underwater landscape was a tunnel construction between a pair of lady's legs; the water was populated by models, dressed as mermaids, complete with fins, arm-length gloves and fishnet stockings. Dalí felt that his attempts to be authentic were frustrated at every turn, with the result that the Fair had been reduced to the 'most monstrous of mediocrities'. In his paper, he harshly criticized the

The Face of War *(Le Visage de la Guerre)*, 1940 (Musée Boymans van Beuningen, Rotterdam). The painting depicts a Spanish cadaver half-devoured by vermin. The brown tonality emphasizes the horror and it is likely that Dalí was thinking of the Spanish Civil war, not of the war which had recently erupted in Europe. Oil on canvas. 64 x 78 cm

'middle-men of culture' who had 'come between the creator and the public'.

Dalí returned to Paris, but he was soon forced to leave. The Germans were close to invading the city and he moved with Gala to Arcachon, just north of Bordeaux, close to the Spanish border. His most famous paintings of this period are *Visage of War* and his unfinished *Portrait of Gala*. He also began to draft his autobiography *The Secret Life of Salvador Dalí* during the eight months spent here. By August 1940, Dalí had again departed for the United States and this time he did not return for eight years. He completed his autobiography during 1941 at the country estate of Caresse Crosby, in Virginia. During the same year, a first retrospective exhibition of his work opened at The Museum of Modern Art in New York. Forty-three paintings and seventeen drawings were put on show, spanning his entire artistic career, from the works of his early youth to his most recent paintings. The museum catalogue featured on its cover Dalí's *Soft Self-Portrait with Grilled Bacon,* which the artist described as 'an anti-psychological self-portrait'. This was quite the antithesis of his previous approach. 'Instead of painting the soul, that is to say, what is within, I painted the exterior, the shell, the glove of myself.' Other new canvases shown at the exhibition, such as *Family of Marsupial Centaurs, Invisible Bust of Voltaire* and *Slave Market* also demonstrated the turning point in his art. Dalí had begun to allow classical influences to seep in. He simplified his subjects and was increasingly attentive to design, balance and precise technique. One critic who commented on the retrospective in the *New Yorker* newspaper predicted correctly that, from this point onwards, Dalí would pay more attention to the conscious rather than the subconscious mind.

The New York exhibition subsequently travelled to eight of America's major cities, securing Dalí's fame and wealth. It was at this time that Breton christened the artist 'Avida Dollars', an anagram of Dalí's name he had devised in reaction to the apparent ease with which Dalí had divorced himself from his Surrealist colleagues and his Spanish roots with the express purpose of making money. Dalí was far too busy to be in any way disturbed by the criticism. He remained fiercely creative until the end of the war, collaborating on jewellery designs with the Duc de Verdur and painting a large number of society portraits for unprecedented sums of money, including those of Mona Harrison Williams, Dorothy Spreckels and Helena Rubenstein. He published *The Secret Life* and wrote his first novel, *Hidden Faces*. He also designed the sets and costumes for several ballets, including *El Café de Chinitas, Colloque sentimental* and *Tristan Insane.* The vast increase in his popularity was largely due to the fact that he took full advantage of the wartime social climate of unrest which allowed the non-traditional to flourish.

Atomic Mysticism on Canvas

The portrait of Dalí's wife which he began in 1944 and named *Galarina,* may be considered the climax of his 'purely' classical paintings. At this juncture, his style was moving towards a coalescence of three distinct influences – classicism, spiritualism and nuclear science. It took Dalí over a year to complete the canvas *Galarina,* whose subject he compared to Raphael's 'La Fornarina'. The portrait was painted at a time when Dalí claimed to have discovered for the first time the real way to paint, and has been linked by the artist to the later canvas *Leda Atomica,* completed in 1948 – to his need to control his imagination and technique through strict rules and research. Towards the end of the war, Dalí began to display a passionate interest in modern scientific discoveries, especially in the field of nuclear physics. The explosion of the

Portrait of Styler-Tas or Melancholy (Berlin National Gallery). Dalí painted this portrait while on a trip to Hollywood in 1945. It was heavily influenced by the portrait of the Duke of Urbino, painted by the fifteenth-century artist Piero della Francesca. Oil on canvas. 65.5 x 86 cm

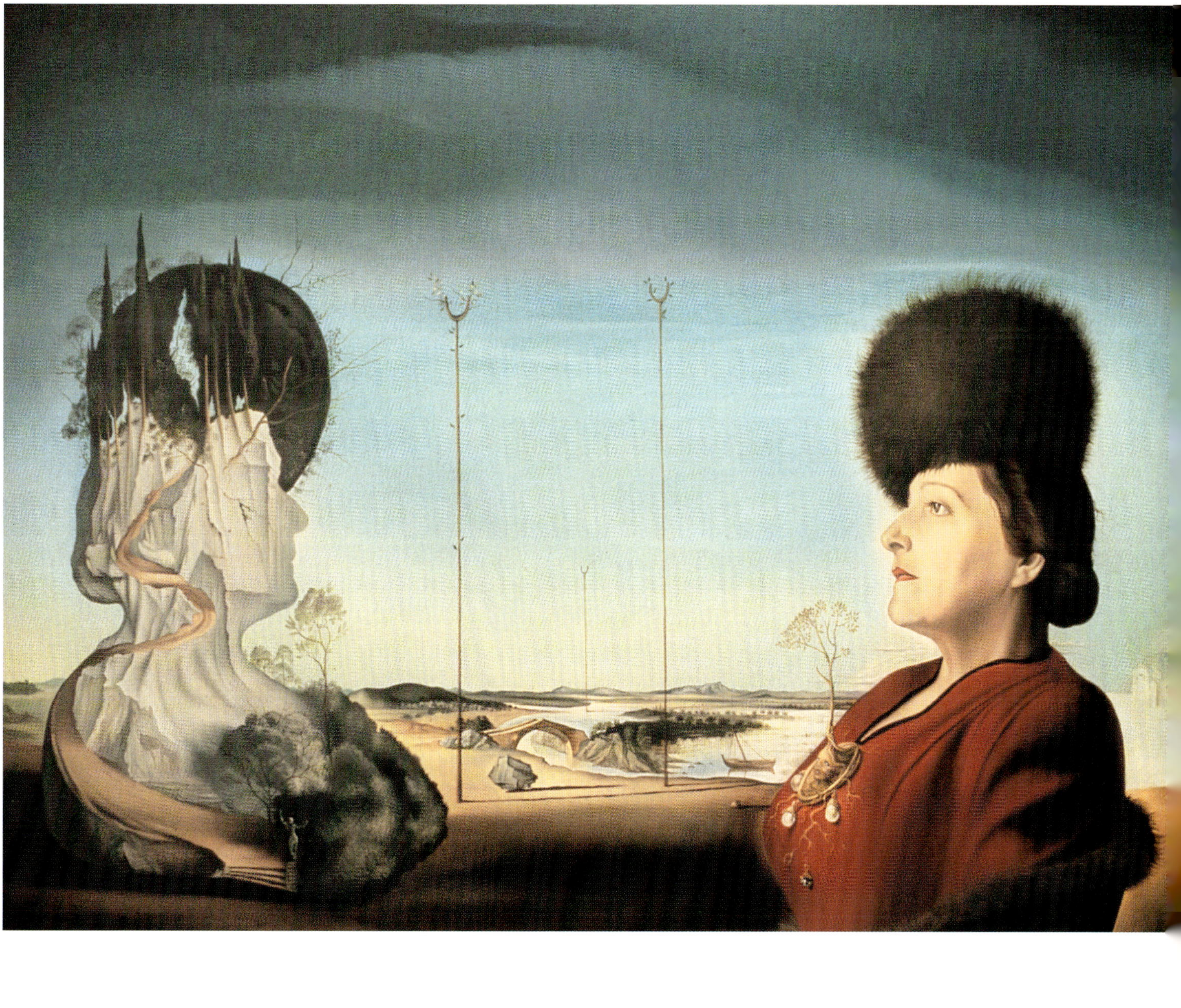

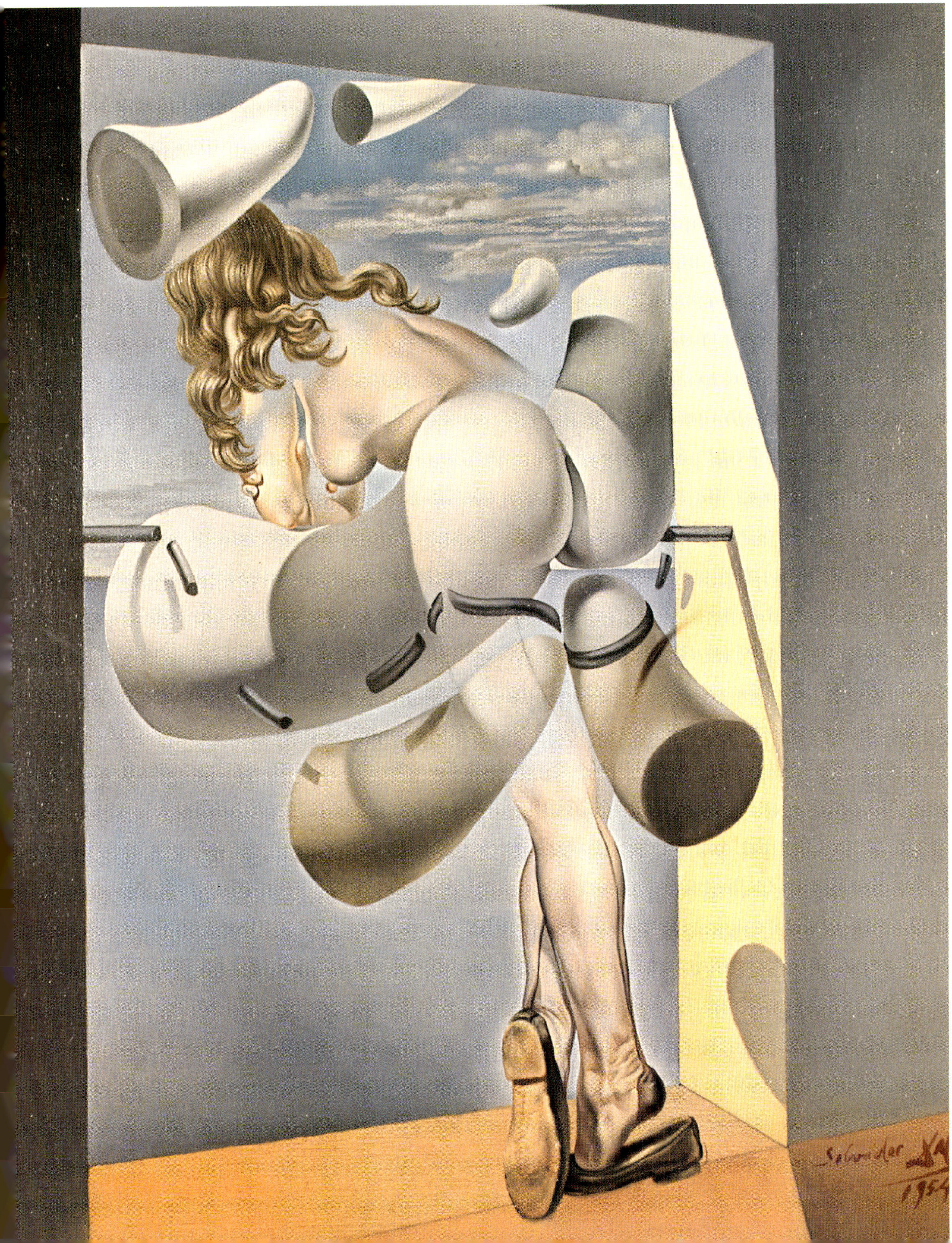

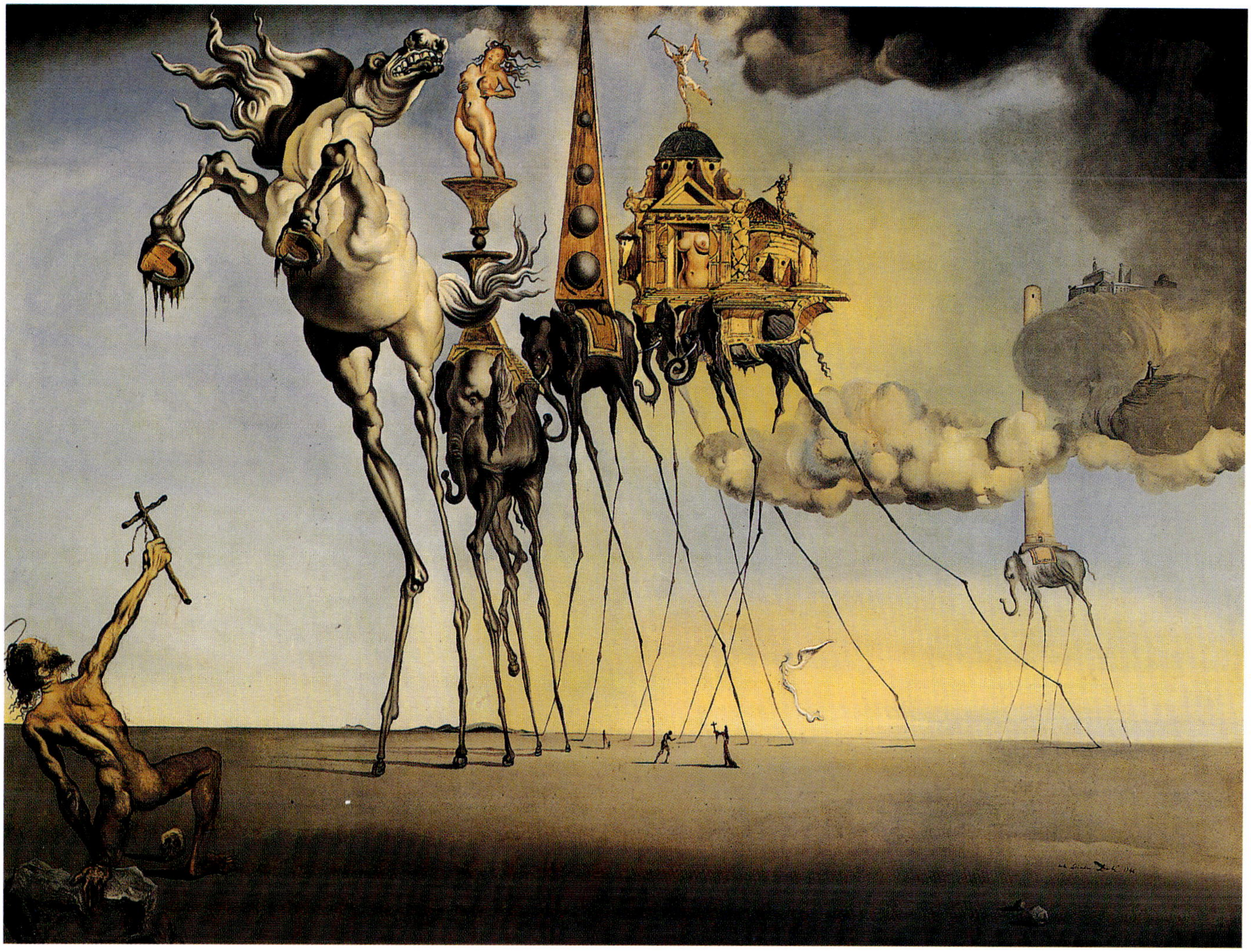

atom bomb in Hiroshima in August 1945 had a profound impact on him, leading him to introduce a scientific topicality into his art as the atom became more and more crucial to his thinking. A number of paintings of this period feature dematerialized objects and representations of the mushroom-shaped atomic cloud, including *Atomica Melancholica*, *The Three Sphinxes of Bikini* and *Dematerialization near the Nose of Nero*. 'My ideas were ingenious and abundant,' he wrote in *Comment on deviant Dalí*, 'I decided to turn my attention to the pictorial solution of quantum theory, and invented quantum realism in order to master gravity. I painted *Leda Atomica*, a celebration of Gala, the goddess of my metaphysics, and succeeded in creating "floating space". I visually dematerialized matter; then I spiritualized it in order to be able to create energy.'

Before painting *Leda Atomica* Dalí began to research the rules of divine proportion as set out by the fifteenth century Italian monk, Fr Luca Pacioli. He also formed a liaison with the famous mathematician, Prince Matila Ghita, who instructed him on the correct mathematical arrangement for the parts of this latest Gala portrait. The three

The Temptation of Saint Anthony *(La Tentation de Saint Antoine)*, **1946** (Brussels Museum of Fine Art).
The intercession between heaven and earth is symbolized here by elephants with elongated, spindly legs. The saint is tempted by power, represented by the horse, and by the flesh, illustrated by the naked female torso and the phallic tower. Oil on canvas. 89.7 x 119.5 cm

Opposite:
Young Virgin Auto-Sodomized by Her Own Chastity, 1954 (Playboy Enterprises, Los Angeles). This painting is a fusion of Dalí's erotic and mathematical concerns, a good example of his belief that 'after Freud it is the outer world, the world of physics, which will have to be eroticized and quantified'. Oil on canvas. 40.5 x 30.5 cm

canvases, *Raphaelesque Head Exploding, Galatea of the Spheres* and *Young Virgin Auto-Sodomized by Her Own Chastity,* painted during the period 1951–5, are further outstanding examples of Dalí's commitment to mathematical theories of composition and his fascination with the particles of matter. The last of these three, together with *Paranoiac-critical Study of Vermeer's Lacemaker,* completed in 1955, explore Dalí's peculiar obsession with the rhinoceros horn as an example of a perfect 'mathematically self-perpetuating logarithmic spiral'. Vermeer's talent for photographic realism had appealed to Dalí from a very early age. He was now convinced that a 'logarithmic perfection' had guided the hand of the artist and his paranoiac-critical interpretation of *The Lacemaker* resulted in the need 'to make the Lacemaker explode in the form of rhinoceros horns'.

The Religious Works

Dalí described his peculiar brand of mysticism as a combination of nuclear, hallucinogenic and religious elements. In particular, he wished to impregnate his 'atomic' art with a revival of Spanish mysticism, which he loosely defined in a series of short sentences as 'the profound intuitive knowledge of what is, direct communication with the all, absolute vision by the grace of Truth, by the grace of God'. He set out to 'demonstrate the unity of the universe, by showing the spirituality of all substance' and maintained the belief that 'heaven was located in the breast of the faithful'. A number of canvases of this period have a predominantly religious theme, founded on Roman Catholic beliefs, through which Dalí set out to demonstrate his convictions. He had been surrounded by pious women throughout his childhood and had been obsessed for many years with the grandeur and ostentation of Catholicism. He had attempted long before now to explore the splendour of Catholic myths through his art. The attempted collaboration with Luis Buñuel on the film *L'Age d'Or* in 1930 was followed by the need to return repeatedly to the Catholic religion as a source of inspiration for his work. As early as 1933, Dalí had displayed a particular fascination for Jean-François Millet's *The Angelus* , a canvas he had first seen while attending the Christian Brothers' school, and he painted several adaptations of the work. The first of the most popular of his overtly religious paintings, *The Temptation of Saint Anthony,* appeared in 1946, followed by *The Madonna at Port Lligat* in 1950, *Christ of Saint John of the Cross,* in 1951, and *The Sacrament of the Last Supper,* in 1955. The culmination of this impressive series was one of the artist's best-known pictures, *The Ecumenical Council,* painted in 1960.

Dalí's obsession with religious themes was unacceptable to a great number of people who had come to admire his work over the

The Ecumenical Council, *(Le Concile Oecuménique),* 1960 (Salvador Dalí Museum, St Petersburg, Florida). Several narrative strands are pulled together in this giant canvas measuring 302 x 254 cm. Dalí's classical iconography of Christianity is often depicted against the background of his homeland. Both he and Gala are painted here in a style of 'handmade photography'. Oil on canvas.

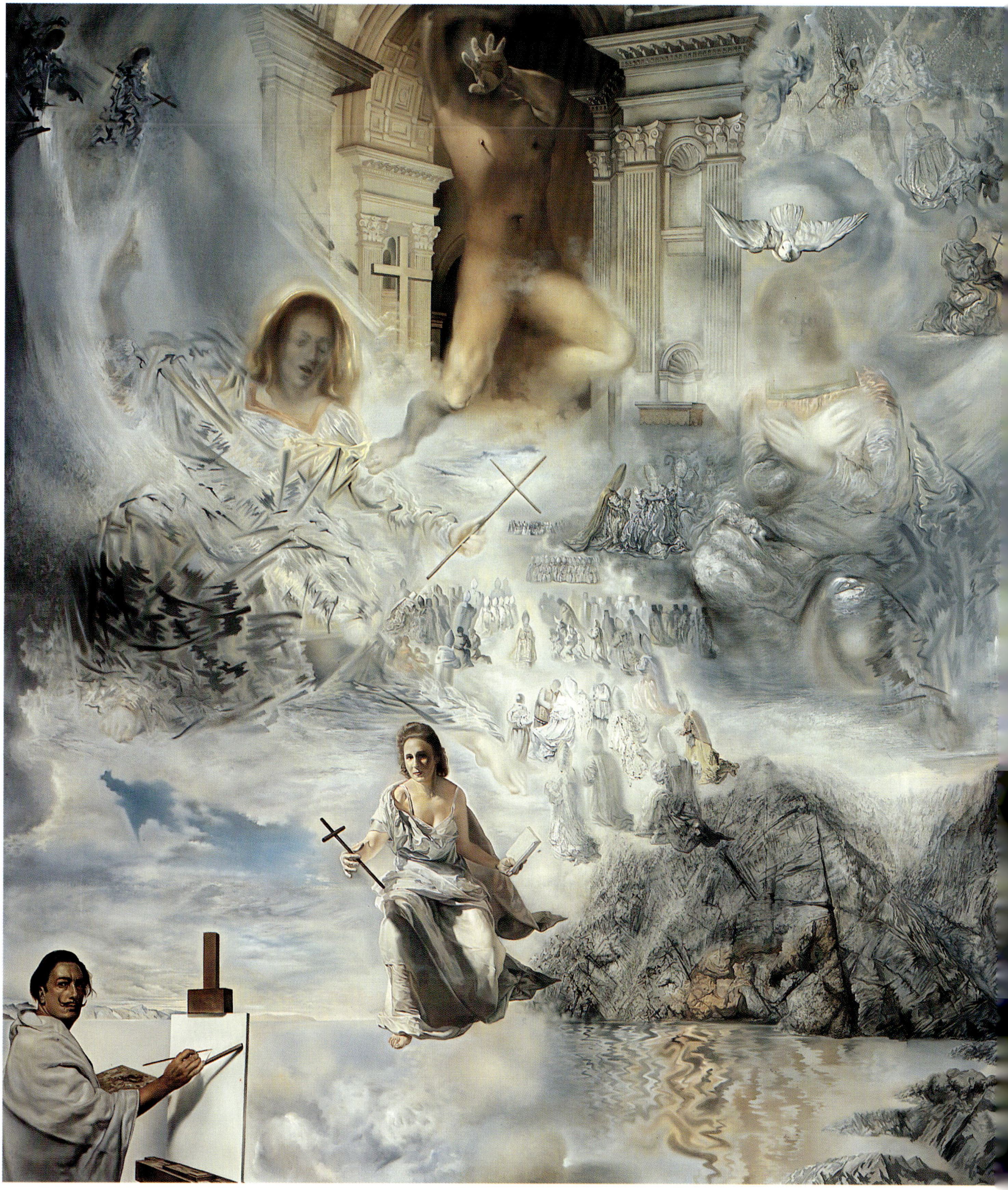

Opposite:
The Madonna of Port Lligat, 1950 (The Minami Museum, Tokyo). Dalí presented this canvas to Pope Pius XII in November 1949. The central image is that of the Virgin Gala whose torso contains a tabernacle. In front of her, the boy Jesus stares into another tabernacle. Oil on canvas.

years. Edward James, Dalí's English patron, acknowledged that *The Madonna at Port Lligat* was 'technically accomplished and laboriously executed' but criticized the religious posturing and hypocrisy behind its conception. 'Nobody could believe,' he wrote to Dalí, 'that there is a grain of religious sincerity in the overtures which you are now making to the Roman Catholic Church.' André Breton was of a similar opinion and openly ridiculed the mercenary nature of 'the personality who recently returned to the bosom of the Catholic church ... and who nowadays quotes letters of congratulation and the approval of the Pope'. Dalí never set himself up as a devout Catholic. He did not attempt to obscure the fact that he borrowed the artistic ideals of the Renaissance for his own explorative purposes. His understanding of mysticism was not a straightforward matter. The iconography of Renaissance paintings held a fascination for him, but his own adaptation of religious subjects was, necessarily, a peculiar blend of agnosticism and Catholicism. Dalí's analysis of *Christ of Saint John of the Cross* elucidates this distinctive quality of his religious work:

> *It began in 1950 with a cosmic dream I had, in which I saw the picture in colour. In my dream it represented the nucleus of the atom. The nucleus later acquired a metaphysical meaning: I see the unity of the universe in it – Christ! Secondly, thanks to Father Bruno, a Carmelite monk, I saw the figure of Christ drawn by St John of the Cross; I devised a geometrical construct comprising a triangle and a circle, the aesthetic sum total of all my previous experience, and put my Christ inside the triangle.*

The Sacrament of the Last Supper *(La Cène)* (National Gallery, Washington). For this large canvas, Dalí took a religious theme and constructed his painting around the architectural form of the twelve pentagons of the dodecahedron and around the geometric elements of the number twelve. It met with a highly controversial response when it was completed in 1955. Oil on canvas. 167 x 267 cm.

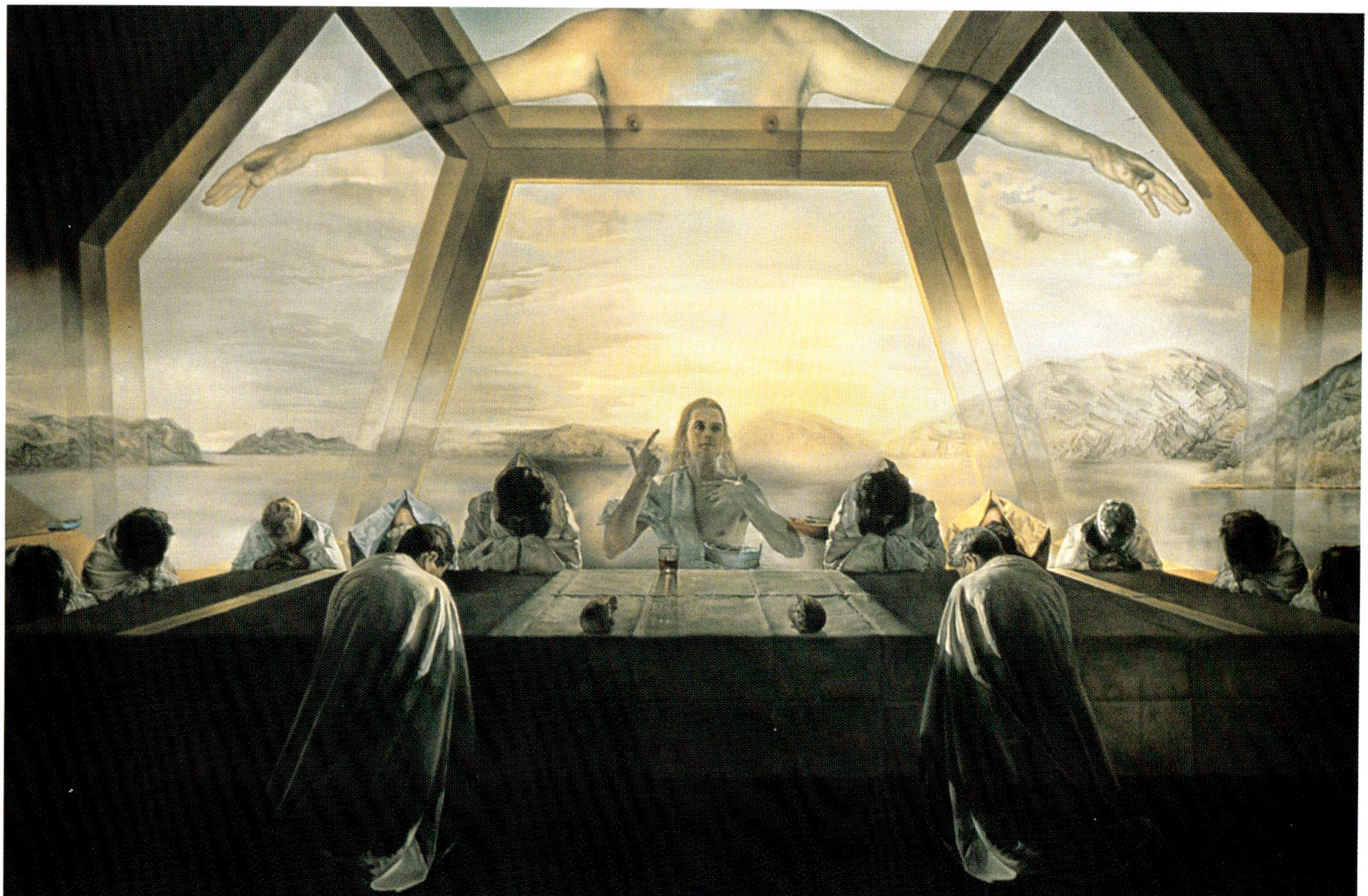

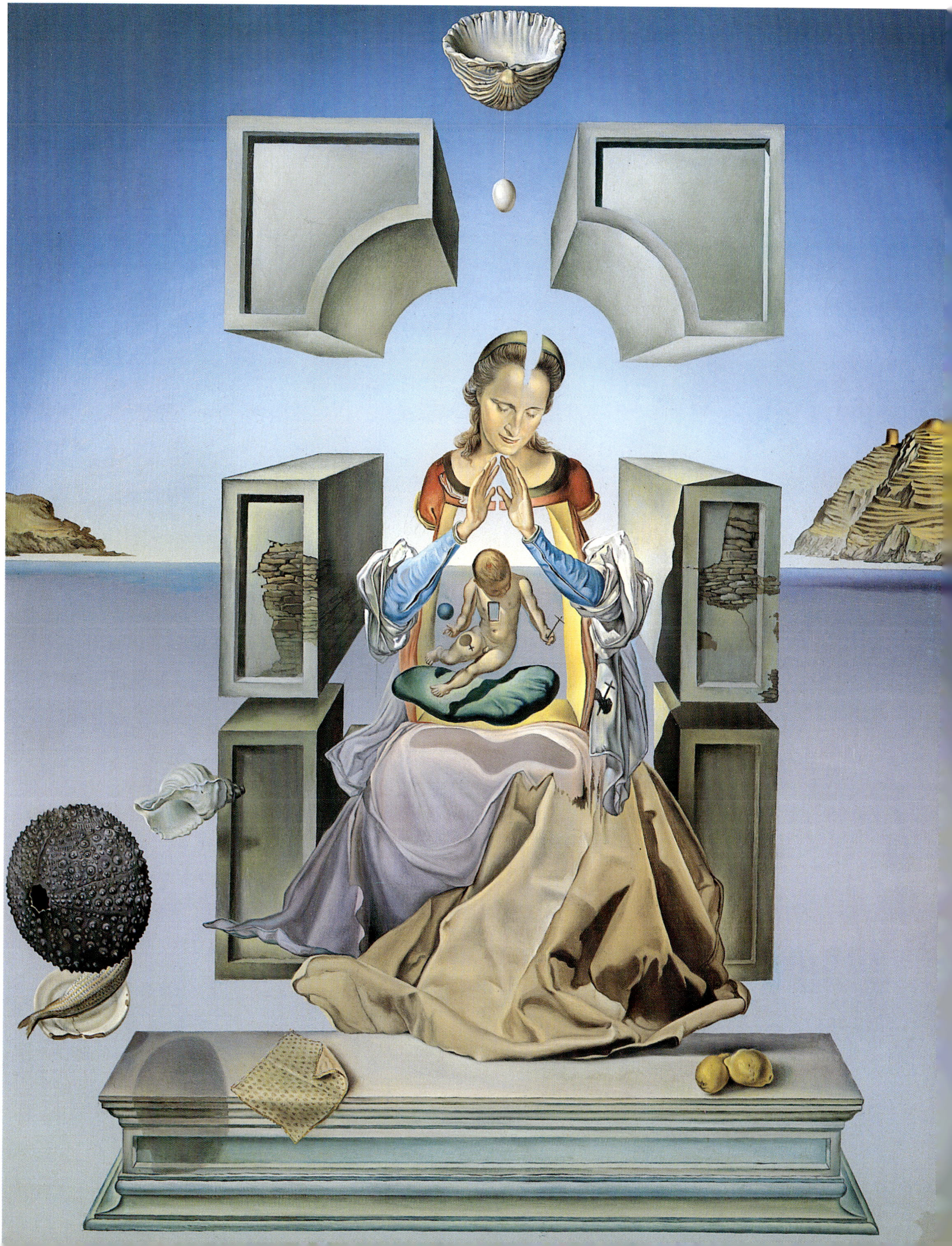

Dalí remained tirelessly prolific even as a mature artist. By 1957, at the age of fifty-three, his paintings revealed yet another decisive shift in subject matter and style, as he moved away from religion towards patriotism and began to introduce a technique of 'corpuscular' painting. Praise for the fatherland now became the central theme of his paintings and it was explored against a background composed of hundreds of minute 'corpuscular' brush strokes. This new method was in keeping with the quantum theory of light, defined as a stream of minute particles. Dalí's first enormous epic composition completed in 1957 was entitled *Santiago el Grande.* It depicts Saint James of Compestela, the patron saint of Spain, in a characteristic style of 'hand-made photography'. This picture was followed by two other canvases of similarly large museum dimensions, *The Discovery of America by Christopher Columbus*, and *The Great Battle of Tetuan.* Both Gala and Dalí appear in the Christopher Columbus canvas, perhaps his best known of this period. The painting depicts the young Columbus being welcomed on the shores of America by Saint Narcissus, the patron saint of Girona. Gala is shrouded in white and represents the Immaculate Conception. She appears on a giant standard which Columbus is reputed to have planted in the ground upon his arrival in the New World. Dalí is the monk kneeling with a crucifix in the lower foreground of the picture.

The unrelenting caprices of Dalí's creative spirit are far too numerous to mention here. Until his death in 1989 at the age of eighty-five, he maintained an enormous artistic output and a high public profile. Two of Dalí's later outstanding canvases were *Tuna Fishing,* painted in 1967, and *Hallucinogenic Bullfighter,* which took two years to complete, between 1968 and 1970. He continued to astound the art world with the scope of his imagination and the passion with which he approached each new enterprise. Dalí was never shy of contemporary art movements, but embraced every opportunity for liberal experimentation. The majority of younger modern artists found it difficult to keep apace with this mature artist who moved rapidly from Pop art, to psychedelic art, to hyperstereoscopic painting, to holograms, to any form of artistic expression which held his attention. In later life, he deliberately continued to feed his audience's appetite for scandal and was thrilled by the invention of television, which became for him the perfect vehicle to expose himself to an even larger audience. By the time he died, Dalí had unequivocally established himself as one the twentieth century's most esteemed artists and intellectual figures. Controversial, extravagant, eccentric, insane, obscene, progressive – Dalí defies categorization. His allegiance was to himself and to the belief in his own genius. His huge success stemmed from the fact that he never once wavered in this belief throughout the course of a long, eventful artistic career.

The Discovery of America by Christopher Columbus, 1958-9
(Salvador Dalí Museum, St Petersburg, Florida). The unity of the Fatherland preoccupied Dalí as a theme from the late 1950s onwards. Oil on canvas. 410 x 284 cm

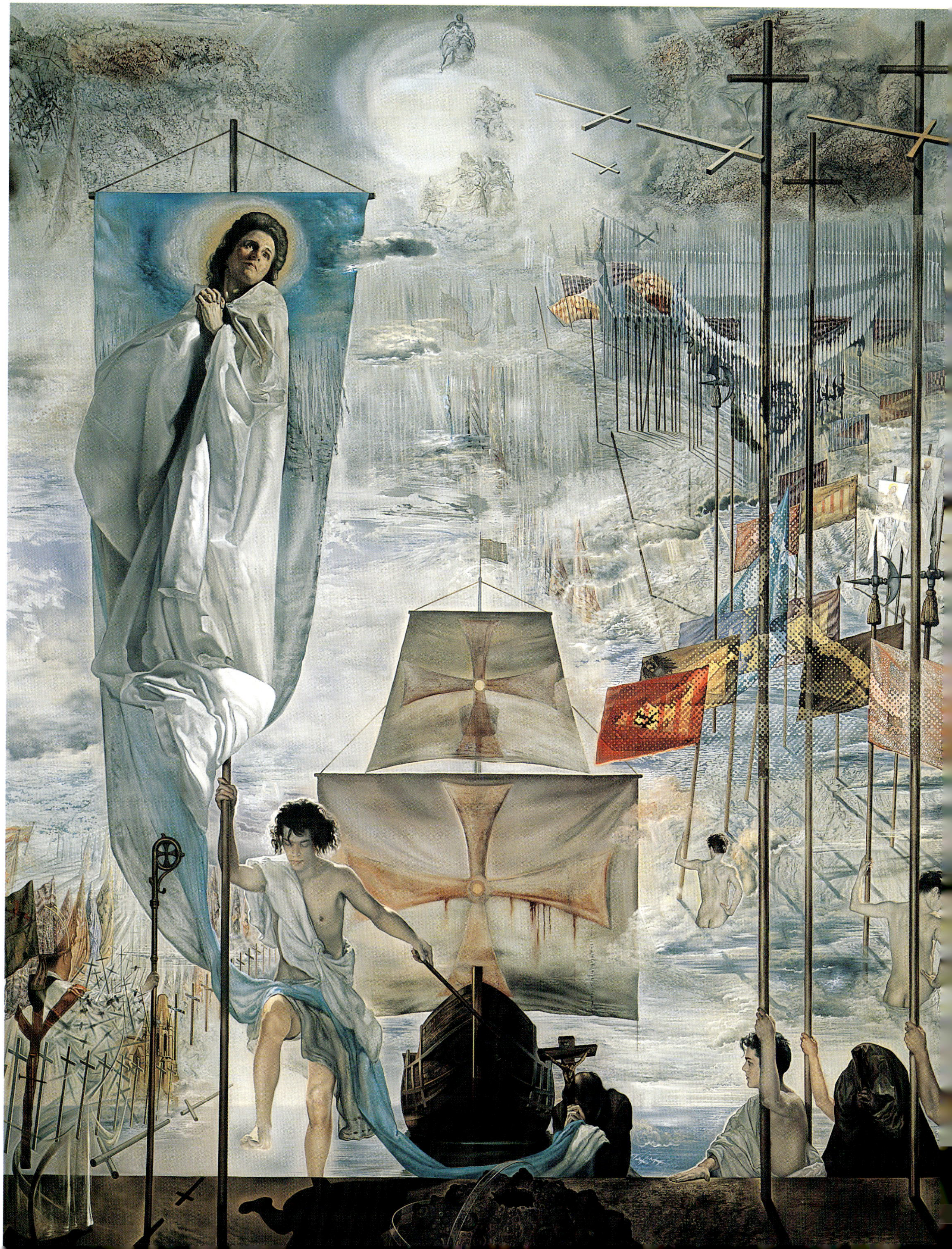

INDEX

Ades, Dawn, 47
Alberti, Rafael, 22
Allegory of an American Christmas, 20
Angelus (Millet), 74
Annunciation, The, 13
Apollinaire, Guillaume, 28
Apparatus and Hand, 31, 32, 35
Aragon, Louis, 28, 59
Arcachon, 70
Arp, Hans, 38
Arrival, The, 11
Atmospheric Chair, 56, 59
Atomica Melancholica, 73
Average Fine and Invisible Harp, The, 56

Bacchanale, 48, 68
Back View of Cadaqués, 17
Ballet Dancer, The, 61
Barcelona, 10, 11, 28, 31
Basket of Bread, 25
Bataille, Georges, 50
Battle of Tetuan, The, 78
Bello, Pepin, 19, 22
Birth of Liquid Anguish, The, 28
Birth of Liquid Desires, The, 30
Bleeding Roses, The, 50
Bosch, Hieronymous, 20
Bouquet of Flowers, 23
Braque, Georges, 19
Breton, André, 20, 28, 39, 50, 55, 59, 76
Bruixes de Llers, Les (de Climent), 23
Buñuel, Luis, 22, 23, 24, 28, 35, 38, 48, 53, 74

Cadaqués, 17
Cadaqués, Catalonia, 10, 16, 19, 24, 44, 48, 53, 54, 56
Café de Chinitas, El, 70
Carrà, Carlo, 19
Chanel, Coco, 67
Char, René, 28
Chien Andalou, Un, 38-40, 52
Chirico, Giorgio de, 19, 28, 65
Christ of Saint John of the Cross, 74, 76
Composition with Greek Head, 39
Composition with Three Figures, 31
Conquest of the Irrational, The, 26, 56
Crosby, Caresse, 64, 70
Cubism, 17, 19, 20, 22, 31
Cubist Self-Portrait, 20

Dadaism, 13, 28
Dalí, Salvador, Catalonian roots and early years, 10-25; surrealism, 28-41; mental health, 44-50; in love with Gala Eluard, 49-52; difficulties with father, 52-4; Port Lligat, 54-5; development and maturity, 56-9; breach with Surrealists, 59-61; American visit, 64; London, 65-6; exile from Spain, 67-70; classicism, 71-4; religious works, 74-7; 'corpuscular' painting, 78
Dalí y Cusi, Don Salvador, 10, 14, 17, 52-54
Dalmau Gallery, Barcelona, 24, 25, 30
Declaration of the Independence of the Imagination, 69
Degas, Edgar, 14
Dematerialization near the Nose of Nero, 73
Design for Vulcain and Venus, 68
Desnos, Robert, 28
Diary of a Genius, 59
Discovery of America, The, 78
Don Quixote, 25
Dream of Venus, 69
Dream, The, 28
Duchamp, Marcel, 65

Ecumenical Council, The, 74
Eiffel Tower and Louis XIV, 58
Eluard, Paul, 28, 38, 48, 49, 60
Enigma of Desire, The, 44, 46
Enigma of William Tell, The, 52, 53, 54
Ernst, Max, 28, 50

Family of Marsupial Centaurs, 70
Femme Visible, La, 47, 50, 56
Ferrés, Felipa Domenèch, 11
Figueres, 10, 11, 14, 16, 23, 24, 25, 35, 52
Figures on a Beach, 35
First Days of Spring, The, 46
First Manifesto (Breton), 28
Fortuny, Mariano, 16
Freud, Sigmund, 28, 53, 67

Gala (Helena Deluvina Diakonoff), 11, 14, 48-9, 52-77
Galarina, 71
Galatea of the Spheres, 74
Garcias, Pedro, 22
Gasch, Sebastia, 31, 35
Gaudi, Antonio, 10, 56
Ghita, Prince Matila, 73
Ghost of Vermeer of Delft, The, 56
Giacometti, Alberto, 58
Girl Seated Seen from the Rear, 35
Girl Standing at the Window, 24
Goemans, Camille, 38, 48, 50, 64
Great Masturbator, The, 47, 50, 56
Gris, Juan, 19
Guernica (Picasso), 67

Hallucinogenic Bullfighter, 78
Harlequin, 20
Harper's Bazaar, 67
Hidden Faces, 70
Hiroshima, 73
Hitchcock, Alfred, 34
Hitler, Adolf, 60
Honey is Sweeter than Blood, 31, 35

Illumined Pleasures, 46
Imperial Monument to the Child-Woman, 53
Impressionism, 16
Interpretation of Dreams, The (Freud), 23
Invention of Monsters, The, 7, 67
Invisible Bust of Voltaire, 70
Invisible Man, The, 53
Italy, 67

James, Edward, 65-6, 76
Jeu Lugubre, Le, 46, 49, 52, 53

L'Age d'Or, 53, 74
L'Amic de les Arts, 31, 32
L'Amour et la Mémoire, 56
L'Ane Pourri, 35
Landscape at Penya-Segats, 25
Leda Atomica, 71, 73
Levy, Julian, 56, 64
Lobster Telephone, 54
Loeb, Pierre, 35
London, 65
Lorca, Federico Garcia, 22, 23, 24, 25, 31, 67

Madness of Tristram, The, 68, 70
Madonna at Port Lligat, The, 74, 76
Mae West's Face, 64-5
Magritte, René, 38, 48, 65
Man Ray, 65
Manet, Edouard, 14
Mariana Pineda (Lorca), 24
Marx Brothers, The, 34
Metamorphosis of Narcissus, 64, 68
Minotaure, 56
Miró, Joan, 35, 38, 65
Montanyà, Lluis, 35
Montes, Eugenio, 22, 40
Morning Ossification of the Cypress Tree, 32

Neo-Cubist Academy, 31
New York, 20, 56, 64, 68, 70
Noailles, Viscount and Viscountess, 53, 65
Ode to Salvador Dalí (Lorca), 24
Old Age, Adolescence, Infancy, 10
Old Age of William Tell, The, 30, 53
Original Sin, The, 22

Paranoiac Figure, 55
Paranoiac-critical Study of Vermeer's Lacemaker, 74
Parinaud, André, 60
Paris, 14, 19, 24, 34, 38-41, 44, 50, 53, 55, 56, 67, 70
Peret, Benjamin, 28
Persistence of Memory – Soft Watches, 44, 56
Picasso, Pablo, 10, 14, 17, 19, 34-5, 64
Pichot, Ramon, 14, 16, 17
Pierrot and Guitar, 20
Pitarra, Serafi, 28
Port Alguer, 23
Port Lligat, 11, 54-6, 56, 64, 67, 68
Portrait of Gala, 14, 70
Portrait of King Alphonsus, 20
Portrait of Styler-Tas or Melancholy, 71
Portrait of the Artist's Father, 24
Portrait of the Cellist Richard Pichot, 17

Raphaelesque Head Exploding, 74
Renoir, Auguste, 14
Retrospective Bust of a Woman, 39
Reverie, 30
Révolution Surréaliste, La, 28
Revolutionaries without Revolution (Thirion), 49
Rubinstein, Helena, 70

Sacrament of the Last Supper, The, 74, 76
Sacred Heart, The, 53
Salon d'Automne, 14
San Fernando Academy, Madrid, 5, 16-20, 23, 24, 30, 32
Santiago el Grande, 78
Schiaperelli, Elsa, 67
Second Manifesto (Breton), 40
Secret Life of Salvador Dali, 13, 14, 19, 23, 34, 40, 49, 56, 59, 70
Self-Portrait, Figueres, 5
Self-Portrait with the Neck of Raphael, 17
Sentimental Colloquy, 68, 70
Seurat, Georges, 19
Shirley Temple (The Youngest Sacred Monster of the Cinema in her Time), 34
Slave Market, 70
Slumber, 38
Soft Construction with Boiled Beans, 67
Soft Self-Portrait with Grilled Bacon, 70
Spanish Civil War, 67, 69
Spectre of Sex Appeal, The, 56
Study for a Record Sleeve, 41
Sun Table, 19
Surrealism, 13, 28-41, 58, 59-61
Surréalism au Service de la Révolution, 55
Surrealist Landscape, 40

Temptation of Saint Anthony, The, 73, 74
Thirion, André, 49, 61
Three Sphinxes of Bikini, The, 73
Thumb, Beach, Moon and Decaying Bird, 35
Town and Country, 67
Tristan and Isolde, 48
Tuna Fishing, 78
Tzara, Tristan, 38, 60

Veu de Catalunya, La (Benet), 31
Visage of War, The, 69, 70
Vogue, 67

Weaning of Furniture Nutrition, The, 56

Yellow Manifesto, 35
Young Virgin Auto-Sodomized by Her Own Chastity, 73, 74

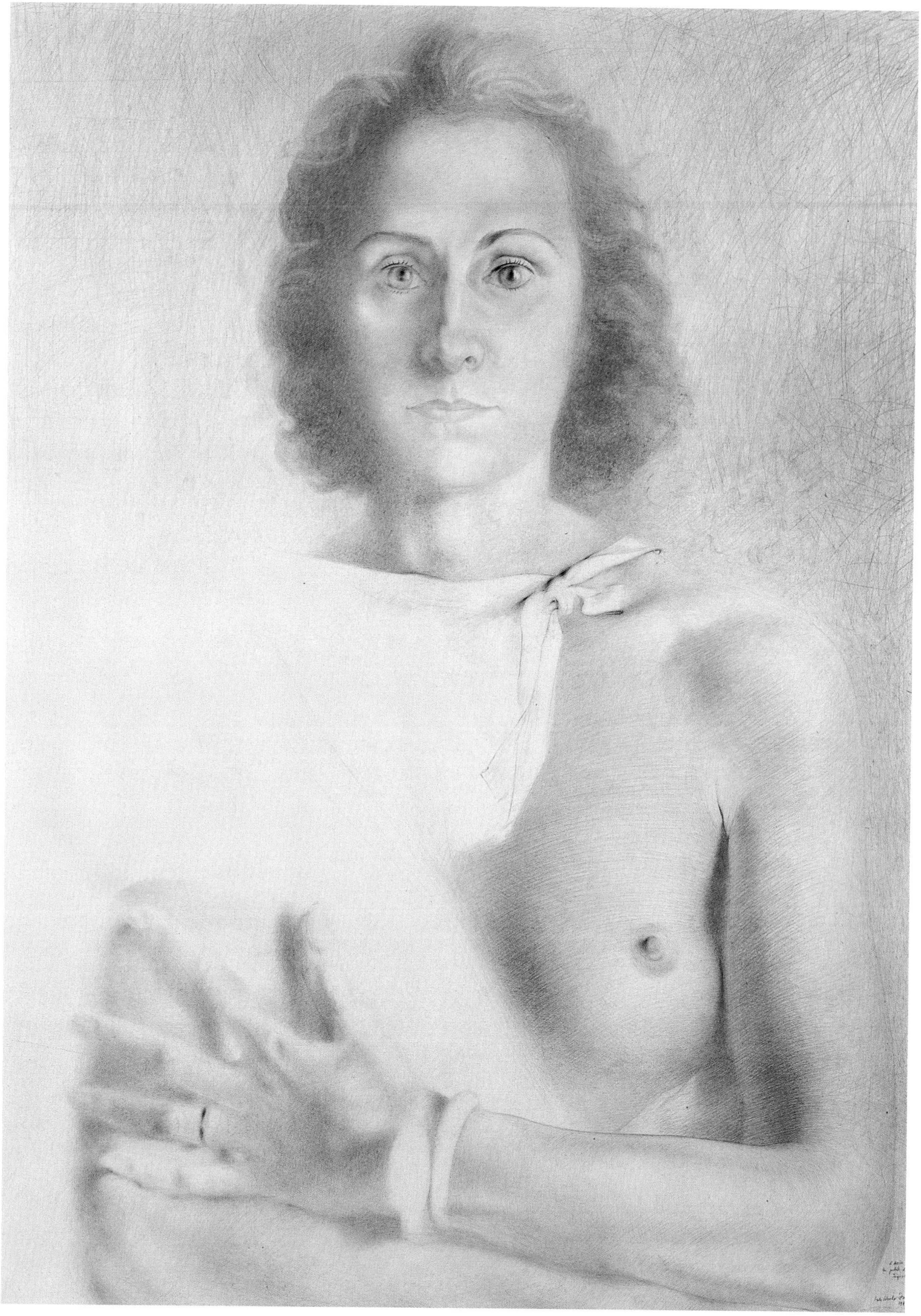

Salvador Dalí. Portrait of Gala, 1941
(Private Collection)

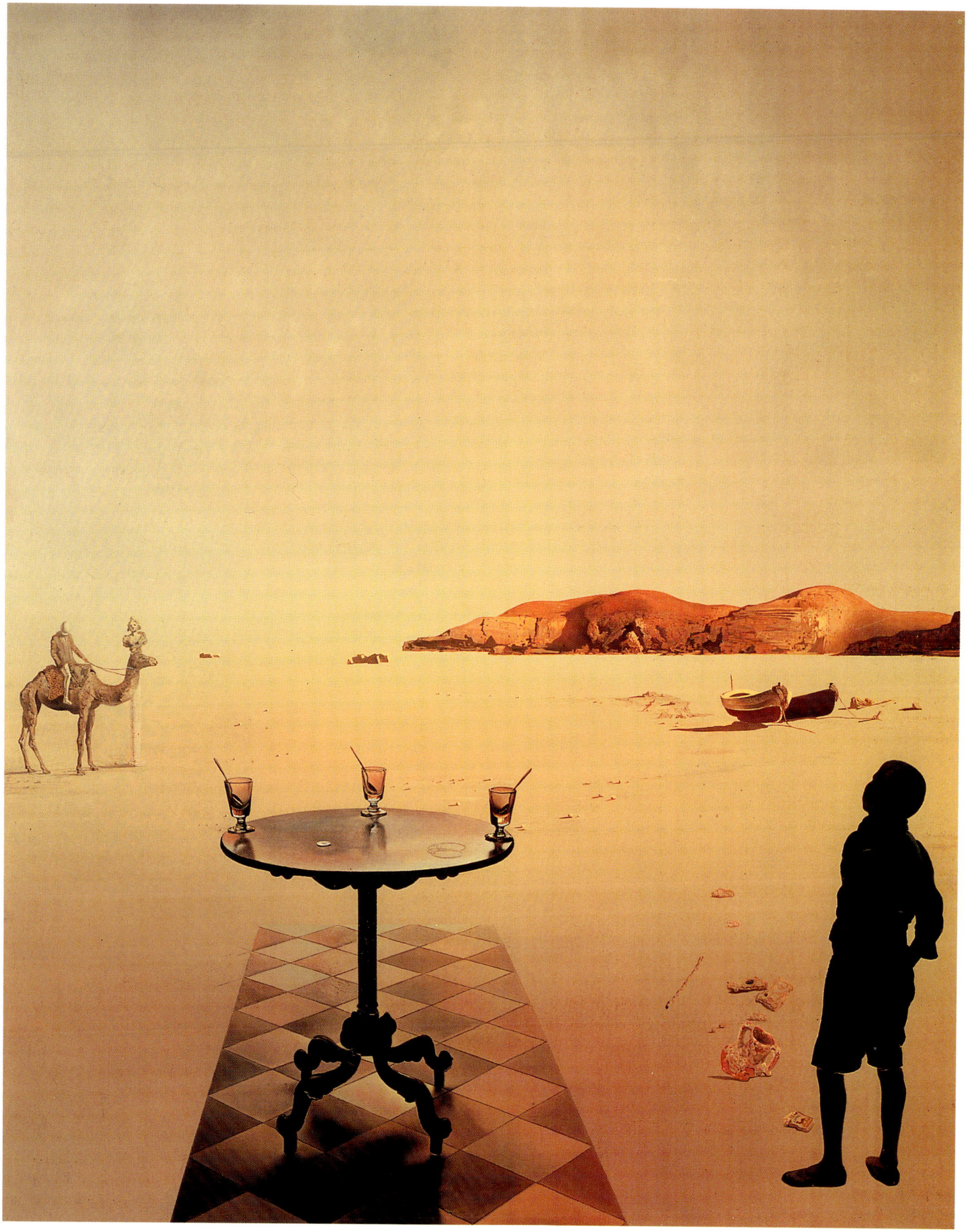

Salvador Dalí. Sun Table ***(Table de Soleil)*****, 1936**
(Rotterdam, Boymans van Beuringen Museum)

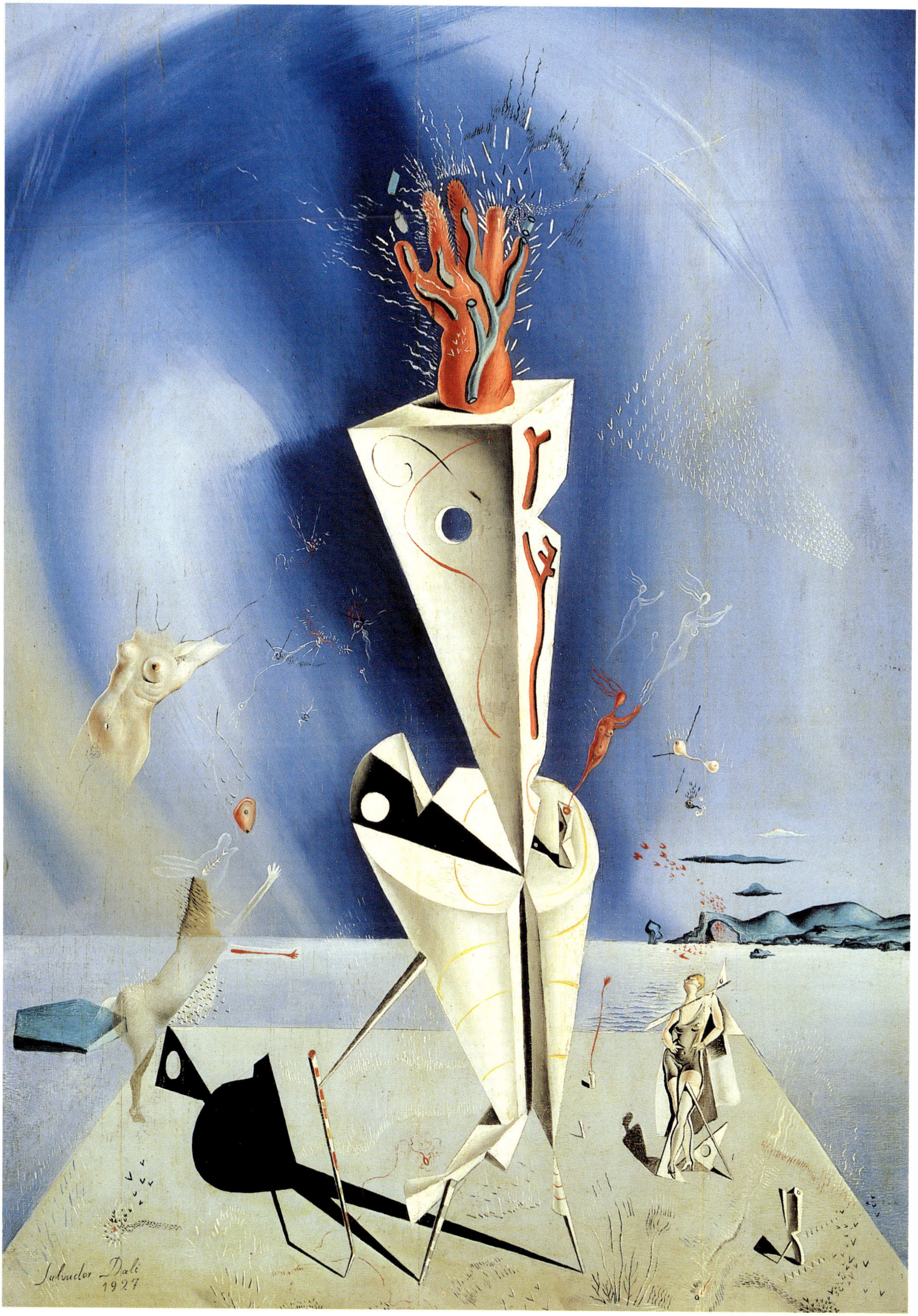

Salvador Dalí. Apparatus and Hand ***(Appareil et Main)*****, 1927**
(Salvador Dalí Museum, St Petersburg, Florida)

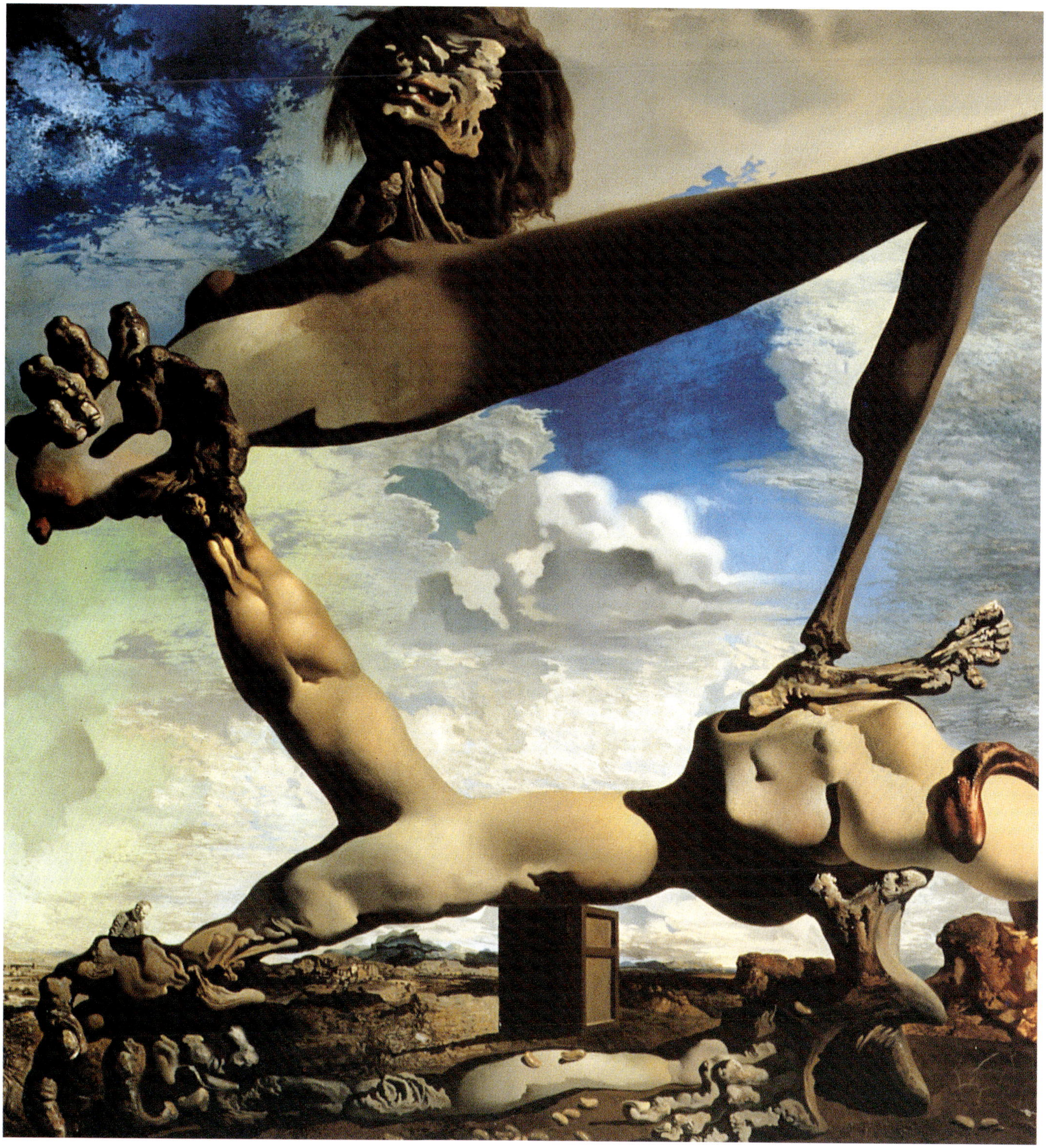

Salvador Dalí. Soft Construction with Boiled Beans: Premonition of Civil War, 1936
(Philadelphia Museum)

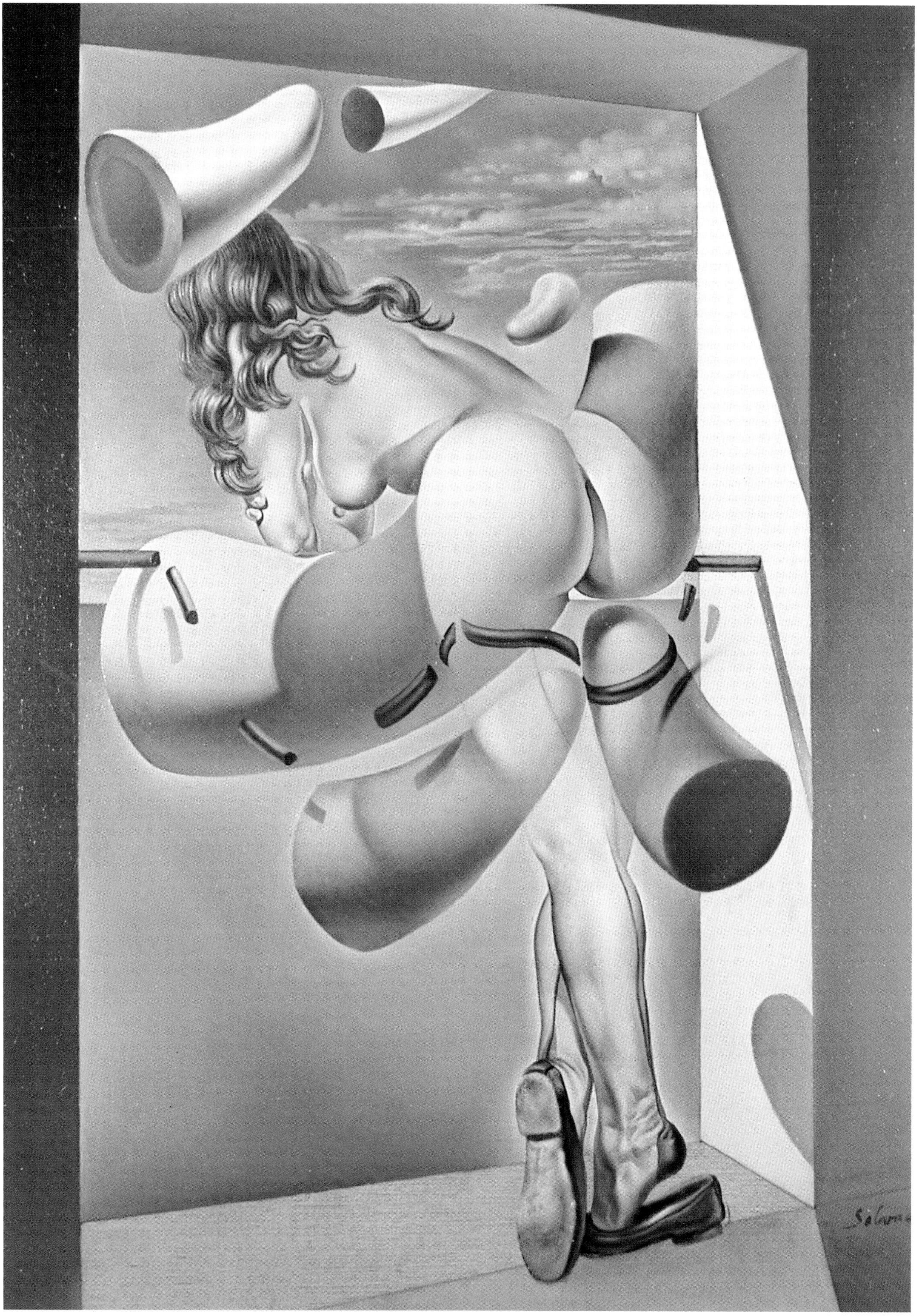

Salvador Dalí. Young Virgin Auto-Sodomized by Her Own Chastity, 1954
(Playboy Enterprises, Los Angeles)

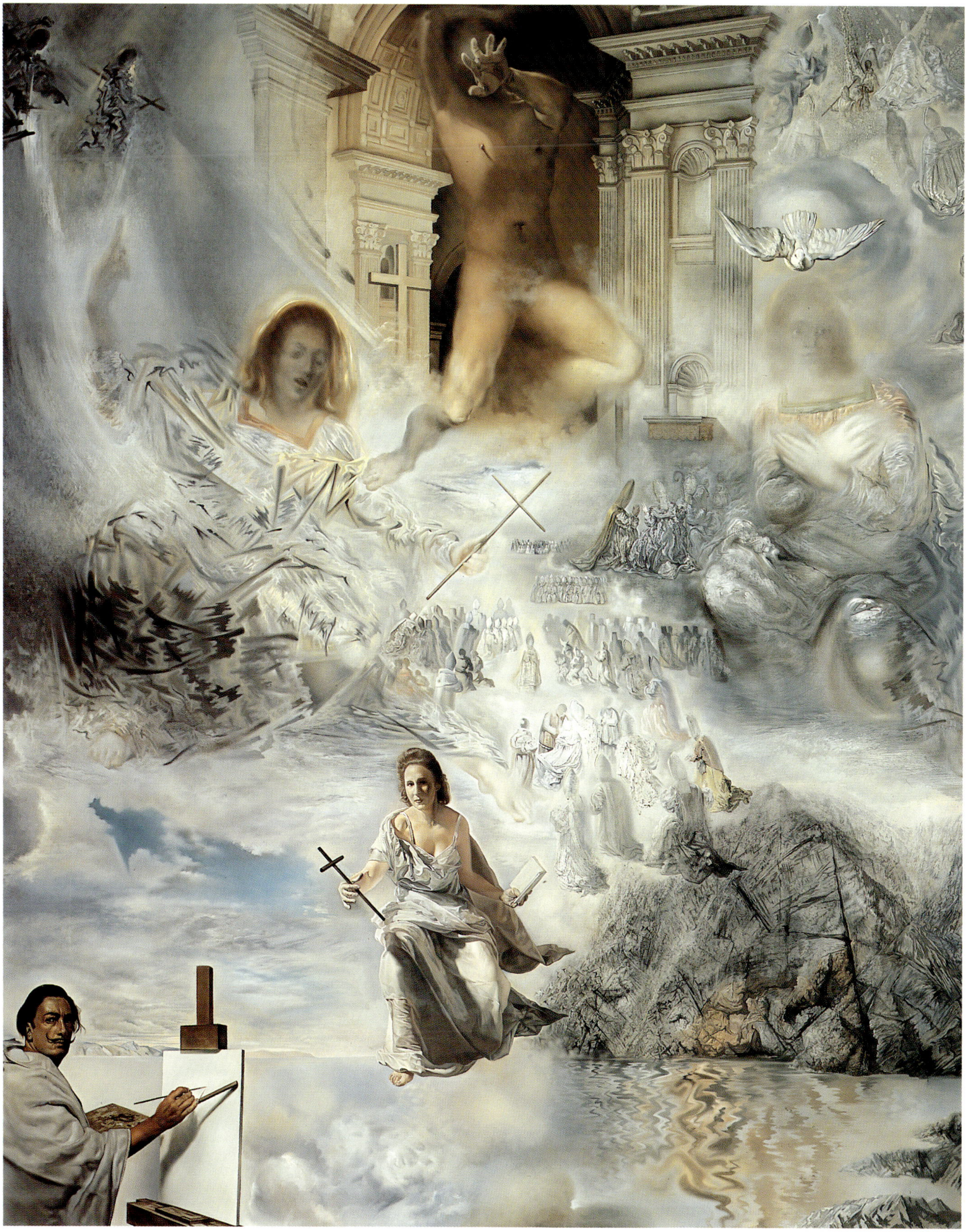

Salvador Dalí. The Ecumenical Council, ***(Le Concile Oecuménique)*****, 1960**
(Salvador Dalí Museum, St Petersburg, Florida)

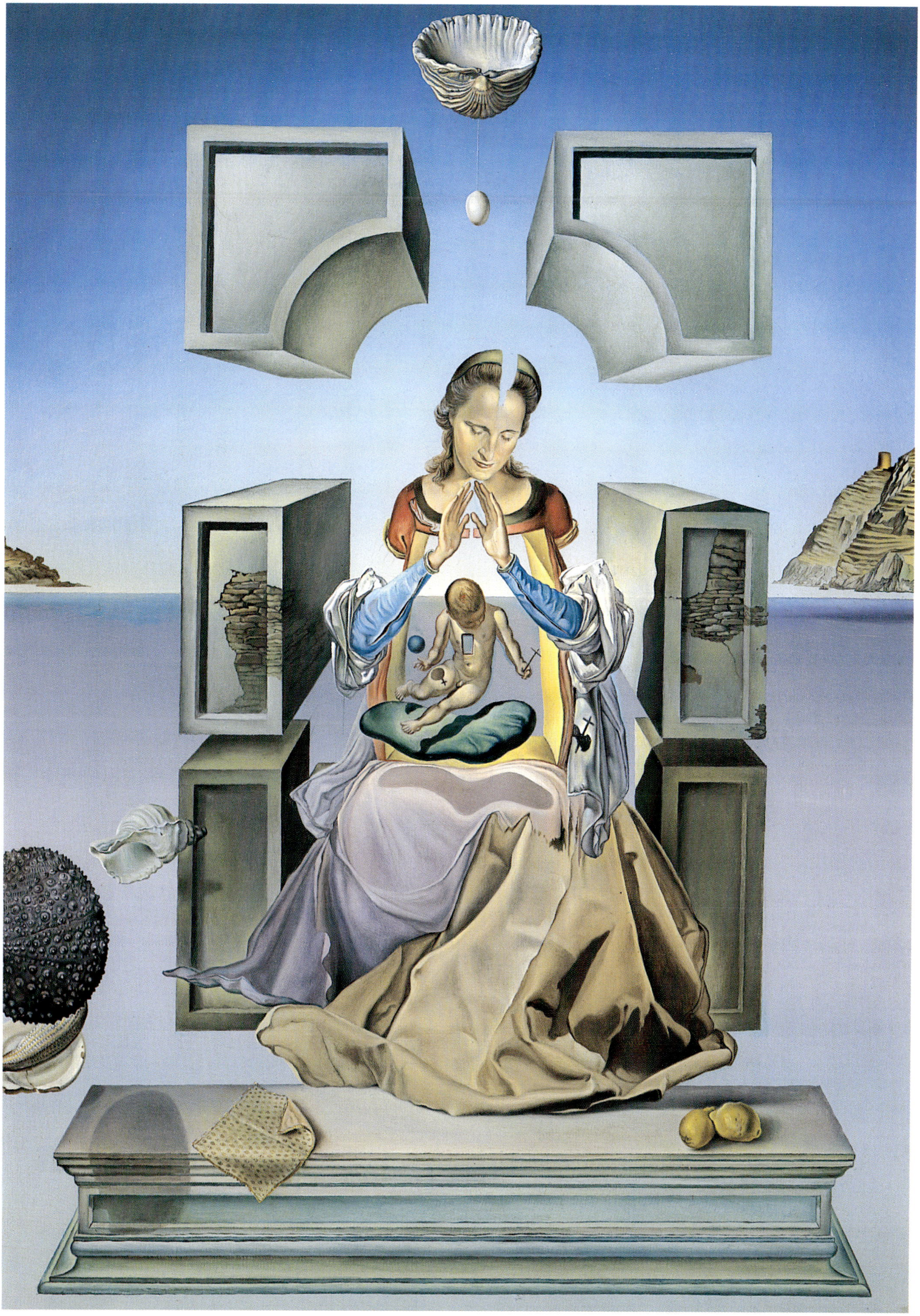

Salvador Dalí. The Madonna of Port Lligat, 1950
(The Minami Museum, Tokyo)

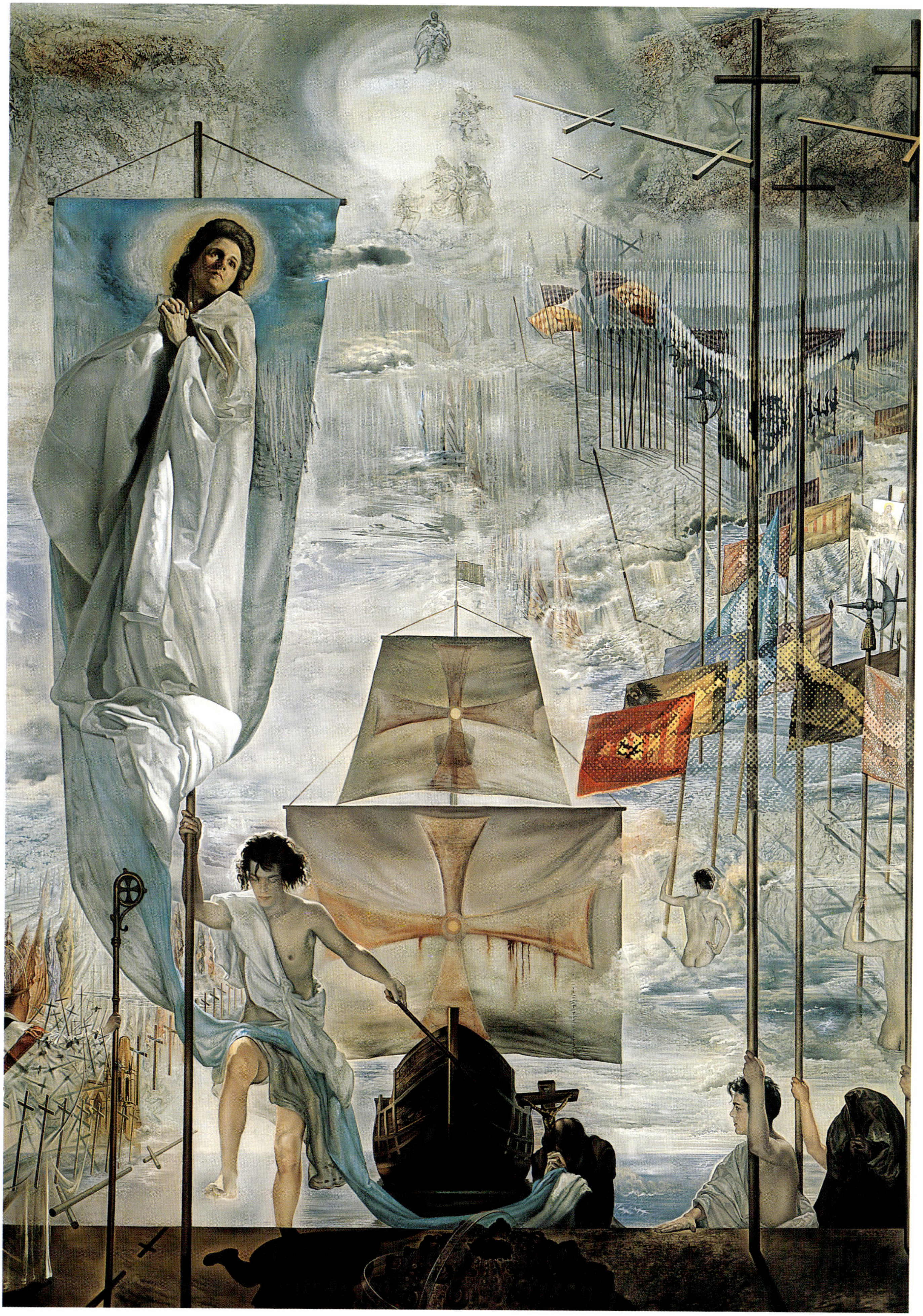

Salvador Dalí. The Discovery of America by Christopher Columbus, 1958-9
(Salvador Dalí Museum, St Petersburg, Florida)